i

DEALING WITH
AND **OVERCOMING**
THE **TRIALS** AND
TRIBULATIONS OF LIFE

AN ENCOUNTER WITH A MASS SUICIDE KILLER

DEALING WITH AND OVERCOMING THE TRIALS AND
TRIBULATIONS OF LIFE
Copyright © 2025 Dr. Rodwell Rillen

ISBN 978-1-967362-84-4 (Paperback)
ISBN 978-1-967362-85-1 (Ebook)
ISBN 978-1-967362-86-8 (Hardcover)

Printed in the United States of America

Statement Of Declaration

PLEASE BE INFORMED THAT ALL NAMES AND /OR CHARACTERS OF INDIVIDUALS REFERRED TO IN MY AUTOBIOGRAPHY ARE DECEASED.

DEALING WITH AND OVERCOMING THE TRIALS AND TRIBULATIONS OF LIFE

As narrated by my late mom, the night of my birth was rainy and fiery. She indicated that type of atmosphere had to have some significance in my life. As I grew to a mental state of awareness about my life when I was about five years old, she kind of filled me in on the previous years of which I had no memory. "You were very cruel to yourself," she said to me one day as a growing child when I was about six years old. I asked her, "How come?" "Well, you would chew on your right small finger whenever you were hungry. You never cried like the regular child." (Having to deal with five other older siblings and being a single mother, she barely had the time to pay full attention to me as a one-year-old toddler). "Suddenly," she said, "I would turn around and see your face bloody and your finger in shreds. So I had to hurry, make your tea, and give it to you to gobble it down while bandaging your finger. Take a look at your right small finger and see how the nail appears shredded." To this day, that mark is still there.

My late mom was very dedicated to all her children. My late father was around, but he never showed much interest in our welfare. He owned a bakery and had another family outside his marriage to my mom. His contribution to nine children (six boys and three girls) with my mom was a big bag of bread every day and $14 per week. The boys took turns in collecting the bread according to age. When it was my turn, I walked about six miles to collect the same. Sometimes, I took a shortcut through the cemetery, which was one of the routes to the bakery. My mom struggled to support us; she left school in the third grade. She always wanted the best for her children. In spite of so many constraints, we never went hungry for a day. Even to this day, it is still puzzling how she managed. We never saw her with another man to indicate she was getting some financial help. I felt so much pity for my mom that one day, after receiving the weekly $14 dollars from my father, I decided to invest it in a three-card game on the street. That was the worst day of my life. I lost every cent of the money. Appealingly, I said to the card dealer, "Mister, my mom would crucify me. Can you give me back part of the money?" "No! And you better get your little behind out of here," was his harsh reply. Devastated, I slowly fixed the big bag of bread slung across my shoulder and sadly made my way back home through the cemetery. "I have to find a good excuse to give the 'old lady,'" I kept saying to myself. We all referred to our mom as the old lady. Then a thought struck me: *Jump into the cemetery's trench water with the bag of bread and claim to be beaten by a gang of guys.* Amazingly, she believed me, and I was saved from a flogging.

My mom was very religious and believed "never to spare the whip and spoil the child." As the sole parent to take care of nine children and being a housewife, to keep us "in line," she had to be stern with us. Of course, I never realized this until I became a grown man. So to satisfy myself, I used to wish bad things to happen to her. As an adult, how regretful have I been of such thoughts. As a growing person during childhood, you don't have the mental capacity to understand adult situations, more so the struggles mothers go through to put food on the table for their kids. Here in America, it is by far easier to provide for children through government programs compared with developing countries, where such programs don't exist and you have to do it all for yourself.

Children in Guyana, formerly British Guiana when I was growing up, started primary school at six years old. We were self-taught at home for about three years before venturing into a primary school of our parents' choice, or should I say parent's choice (mother) because fathers showed little interest in their children's welfare. So like every child's experience, the first day of school was miserable. It took about one week to adjust to the school's environment. Little ABC (first grade) was the name of the class. After one year, if successful, one would be promoted to Big ABC (second grade), then first standard (third grade), and second standard (fourth grade). At that time, kids between nine and ten years old were invited to take a special examination known as the Common Entrance and, if successful, were qualified to attend high school. Next is third standard (fifth grade), then fourth standard (sixth grade), followed by fifth standard (seventh grade), and finally, sixth standard (eight grade). After the eighth grade, a student qualified to go to high school. After completing high school, many graduates would try to get a job. At that time, no colleges were operating in British Guiana. Further studies had to be pursued in foreign countries mainly England, USA, and Canada. Because of personal financial predicament, most individuals had to depend on government scholarships to go overseas for higher education. Education is the top priority of parents in Guyana for their children. Because of this discipline, fear of God and respect for your elders were enforced at an early age.

Having the ability to complete a task once started was a major quality enforced by mothers on their children. Mothers took a keen interest in their children's progress while in school. My mother gave birth to nine children (six boys and three girls) with one man. Children born out of wedlock were looked on as outcasts by society. My mother, even though married to my dad, was actually a single mom working from home, doing cooking, sewing and laundry for friends and relatives. My father never lived at home. He owned a bakery and had a second family (two boys) out of wedlock. The only support we got from him was a big bag of bread and $14 per week. My mom was so disciplined that in spite of her own lack of education (coming out of school in the third grade), she would see all her children through high school, which she had to pay for out of pocket. My father was from Dutch Guiana (Suriname). He came to British Guiana when he was sixteen years old, only knowing how to speak the Dutch language, but learned to speak English over the years. So he wasn't an educated person. Further, he never showed any interest in our upbringing and education; that was about 90 percent of the mothers' job. So my mom controlled us with an iron fist to instill this discipline. We lived on Durban Street in the city of Georgetown, and we were the most feared children on the block, but our mom never knew that about us. She thought we were these good children she was raising because that was the way we behaved when she was at home. She bought fresh food from the market every day, so when she was out trying to do her best to support her children, that was the time we used to create havoc among ourselves and the neighbors' children. On her return, no one would dare mention such behavior to her. Aside from the disciplinary training, everyone was assigned chores which had to be completed early in the morning before going to school and in the evening after returning from school. My responsibilities at seven were taking care of the chickens which we reared for food and cleaning all utensils used by everyone. Taking care of the chickens was fun and no fun. The fun part was seeing them grow from chicks to adult hens and roasters, trying to cure them when they got sick, and retrieving the eggs. The "no fun" part was cleaning the coop where they slept and slaughtering them for cooking. During that time of my life, even though I was subjected to a high level of discipline, it was great fun; I was allowed the freedom of the environment to run around and play with my siblings and many times escaped to play with friends. Yes! Escaped! My mother would tell us that we were many to play with each other and didn't need friends. But that was one of the few times she was wrong. We fought among ourselves as if we were enemies. I was very quiet and acted more violently. As many kids do, you adopt some strange hobbies. Mine was practicing how to throw knives. This culminated in a near-tragic accident. My eldest sister teased me one day (at that time, I had a broken leg and was very miserable most of the time, not being able to move around freely), and with lightning speed, I spun around and threw the bread knife at her which caught one of her long hair plaits and firmly stuck it in the door which she was running toward to escape from me. At that time, I didn't show any remorse. But as I got older and, to this day, as I remembered the scene, I get chilly sometimes knowing that I could have killed my own sister.

We were the most feared children in our neighborhood. We attacked the neighbors' children in an all-out war with bricks and bottles. As a result, my mom was in court many times, answering charges on our behalf because parents were responsible for their children's behavior. So on a particular day, while she was preparing me to go with her to court to answer charges for my brothers splitting open the head of one of the neighbor's children with a rock, I managed to leave the house unnoticed, went to the front gate leading to the road, and saw a crowd of people up the street enjoying the moments of the town drunk who was popularly known as Sagiewang. As I was running up the street to join in the amusement, a large delivery bicycle hit me and sent me flying, resulting in a compound fracture of my left leg. Now all the attention was shifted from the town drunk to me. "I can manage on my own. My mother will take care of everything," I said to a couple of concerned members in the crowd while waiting for the ambulance to arrive. My broken leg nearly resulted in me losing it. An infection resulted without my mom realizing it until one day, my uncle said, "This boy's leg is smelling stink." I was taken to the hospital, and the doctor gave my uncle the bad news of having to amputate my leg to prevent blood poisoning. Well, my uncle wasn't one to accept anything negative initially. He asked the doctor if he can imagine a young child growing up with one leg, so he had to do something to save my leg. The doctor took up the challenge and saved my leg.

All of us (siblings and myself) believed that my mom was some kind of a super person, that she could have cured any ailment or injury we suffered from during our early childhood years. We never saw a doctor; she had previously demonstrated her wisdom with cures for many of the serious diseases and injuries we got. She used herbal medicine. One outstanding, memorable moment occurred when I was about five years of age. The same kids who suffered those serious injuries at the hands of my brothers that my mom was about to answer for in court had caught and stabbed me in the chest with a broken bottle. I run to her with blood squirting from an artery about half an inch from my heart, and she calmly put pressure on the wounded area, got some spider web from the house, and packed it into the wound. Amazingly, the bleeding stopped immediately, and the serious wound was healed in one week. I am constantly reminded of that incident every day when I take a shower as a large scar is still felt in the center of my chest.

My uncle, my mother's brother, was a funny guy. He was more of a father to us than our biological father. He was always there for us. He told us he divorced his wife a couple of days after getting married because he didn't know she was that ugly without her makeup. Again, we were thought poems of respect for each other, such as "Little children love each other, never cause another pain. If your brother speak in anger, answer not in anger again." My uncle would jokingly change it to say, "Little children love each other, never cause another pain. If your brother speaks in anger, kick his ass down the stairs." He worked in the interior of Guyana with a mining company and could only come to see us once per year, at Christmas time, which was the most joyful time of our lives. During that time, performers danced in the streets to the beat of African drums, and steel pan musicians invited the public to dance in the streets to their melodious tunes. But one Christmas season, all this revelry went unnoticed. My uncle invited me to accompany him to purchase a pig from the country area (this was the custom every Christmas for our family) where farmers raised their livestock. It was a rainy day. Much of the farmlands were flooded, and in some of the deep trenches that had bridges, the water overflowed their banks. As we looked and did not find a reasonable purchase, I saw a house on stilts about a hundred yards away, surrounded by water (in many homelands that are flooded, one is able to trudge through the water with long booths). Thinking that this was the situation, I suggested to him that we should try to go over to that house to inquire about the availability of any hogs for sale. He knew that there was a deep trench we had to cross over, but being the jovial one that he was and not knowing that I would have obeyed his suggestion, he said, "You go, and I would follow." Off I went toward the house and walked smack into the trench. Not knowing how to swim, I went down under the water once, then twice, and when I was about to go under the third and final time, he appeared, grabbed my outstretched hand, and pulled me to safety. I never saw him so distraught, realizing that one of his jokes could have cost my untimely demise. So that was the end of the search and the first Christmas we didn't have our garlic and roast pork, which was one of the delicacies my mom prepared for us to enjoy at Christmastime.

At about eight years of age, I developed a passion for the sport of cricket, which is similar to baseball in the way the game is played, but the rules are different. It seemed that I was a natural player of the game, never having to be taught how to play it like other kids. Presently, the game is almost played in all countries of the world, including the United States. Guyana, even though geographically situated in South America, culturally is Caribbean/West Indian. So the West Indies cricket team is represented by all the Caribbean Islands and Guyana today. But when I was a child, all the players were from Jamaica, Trinidad, Barbados, and Guyana. So with the West Indies team being one of the major cricket teams in the world before I was born, I was all for them. At eight, I decided my career in life would be a cricketer playing for the West Indies team. Cricket in Guyana and the Caribbean is like a religion. Whenever there are major games (test matches) between West Indies and other cricketing nations such as England, Australia,

India, Pakistan, and New Zealand, I would spend most of my day listening to radio commentary on the game because television was not present in Guyana. My mom could not have gotten me to do any errands. That was an ordeal for her because the cricket game started at 11:00 a.m. and finished at 5:30 p.m. and lasted for six consecutive days.

Have you ever heard that if a dead person does not want you to be at his/her funeral and you attend, that dead person's face would show annoyance? Well, I have had that experience. One day, while playing a friendly game of cricket in the next-door neighbor's yard during one of my "getaway episodes from chores at home," being the terrific batsman that I was, I gloriously drove the ball that was bowled to me right into the neighbor's window where she was sitting. Two days later, she died from a ruptured blood vessel in the brain because of the shock she experienced from the ball flying at a fast rate of speed toward her. That was devastating to me even though I knew it was an accident. On the day of the funeral, she was displayed for viewing in her yard space. I turned up to the viewing, and behold! I actually saw her face changed to one of annoyance. Seeing that, I bolted from that site and isolated myself at home for about a week, much to the amazement on my mom because she could never find me whenever there were chores to be done.

Later, after my frightening experience with the dead, I was flashing my bat in the schoolyard opposite my home to the astonishment of a crowd that had gathered on the street to see my batting on display. After the game, I was approached by an untidily dressed male individual about 40 years of age, who uttered his amazement to me about my batting display. He invited me to his car and offered me my favorite fruit, banana. But in spite of my love for bananas, I was taught by my mom never to accept anything from strangers. His questions were about my brother's friend who was our next-door neighbor and was being investigated for theft of government funds. So at nine years of age, I thought I was responsible, to an accepted degree, to relay this information to my mom. After asking politely for an excuse, I ran to the house and told my mom about the encounter with the stranger. We told our mom most of everything; she never feared anything or anyone. After dressing-down the stranger with some harsh words, he admitted that he was a police detective. My brother's friends, three of them, had skillfully robbed a government health agency (Ministry of Health) of $28,000. One friend, who was about twenty-two years of age, five feet three inches tall, weighing about 110 pounds, and of mixed race, concocted the idea to forge the signature of the accountant who signed the checks to pay the salaries of employees for the month. The second friend, our neighbor, was about the same size, height, and age but of African heritage. His job was to forge the signature of the accountant, but neither of these guys had the courage or "guts" to cash the check. So they had to get a third person to do the job of cashing the check. In came the third guy. He was of Portuguese decent and about five feet ten inches tall and weighed about 140 pounds. On the eve of the robbery, he came to ask my brother to borrow his unique sports coat, telling him he had a date with a girl and he wanted to impress her with his appearance. So the next day, the day of the robbery, as reported by him, he turned up at the bank looking like some rich dude from high society. He presented the check to the cashier. She looked at it for some time, then told him she will be back soon, and disappeared through the manager's door into his office. Well, it's now clear why a third person with the nerves of steel was needed to cash the check. He stood his ground, being cool, calm, and collective. After about ten minutes, the cashier returned with a smile on her face and asked, "How do you want it?" He replied, "Large bills, please." He calmly placed all of the money in a briefcase and slowly walked out of the bank. It was said to be the perfect robbery. But, as is known, nothing or no one is perfect; and in spite of how good a plan is, there's always a mistake. So since my encounter with the detective from my schoolyard display of my masterly batting, things started to get really interesting with the police investigation. Their suspicion was initiated with the wild spending of two of the three guys. The second guy was a mechanic and lived next door with his parents in an old shingle-type two-story house that had a yard toilet. He barely made ends meet from his salary. He was very friendly with my older brothers and visited our house frequently. Almost immediately after the robbery, he bought a new car with police-type headlights attached to it. Most of the neighbors knew when he was returning home from his nightly activities, being awaken with his flashing headlights early in the morning at about 2:00 to 3:00.

Everyone who was associated with the suspects was targeted by the police for questioning. So one evening, three detectives appeared at our house. My mom, who was about forty years of age, of mixed race, about five feet six inches tall, somewhat fat with curly hair, and of fair skin, loved to sit in a rocking chair by an open window. Our house was built on stilts consisting of large beams of solid wood and had about sixteen stairway steps leading up from the ground to the front door. One detective came up the stairway and knocked on the door. My mom answered the door. "Yes?" The detective identified himself as Ralph and said, "I come to search your house." Sternly, my mom replied, "For what?" He replied, "Stolen property." "Do you have a search warrant?" "Yes." "Where is it?" "In the car." "Well, why are you standing there? Go and get it." He left, somewhat surprised and intimidated by the expression of a woman, and returned with the warrant about fifteen minutes later, accompanied by two other detectives. My mom said, "Before you come into my house, empty your pockets." The leading detective asked, "Why?" "Because the police have a way of finding what is not there and, to be more specific, planting evidence." By that time, we had gathered around my mom, my four smaller siblings from four to eight years of age and me about ten years old. "Mrs. Rillen," referring to my mother, "this is very embarrassing," was the detective's reply. We stood there and saw three grown middle-aged men empty their pockets inside out before they walked through the door. Now these detectives were to be further embarrassed by my mom. She gave us the assignment of monitoring the search by the detectives. "Nothing is behind my schoolbag," shouted my four-year-old brother as one of the detectives fumbled with his schoolbag that was hanging on the wall. The search was extremely embarrassing for the detectives, so after about ten minutes, they left but continued to monitor our home in the following days. One evening, they were back again, this time to arrest my second eldest brother, Andrew (who has recently passed), who was not at home; he had gone to the dentist to extract a bad tooth. While the detective was in discussion with my mom about his whereabouts, my eldest brother, Alden, came out of the room; and frantically, the detective said, "That's him! I thought you said he wasn't at home." At that same moment, Andrew came up the stairway, returning from the dentist. "No! That's him," confusingly exclaimed the detective. Angrily, my mom asked him, "Who the hell did you come to arrest?" After looking carefully at the striking resemblance of my two brothers and at a portrait he had of Andrew, the detective decided that Andrew was "their man." Now it is known that the police uses violence on suspects to get evidence from them and to say things they want to hear. In fact, they had beaten the third person in the robbery that withdrew the money from the bank to get information about my brother's association with the two other suspects. As they placed Andrew in handcuffs, my mother angrily addressed the detectives, "If my son comes back with a single scratch on him, I will see that all of you lose your jobs." Ten minutes later, my bother returned home; and when my mom inquired what happened, he told her that the detectives were so scared of her that they decided she wasn't the kind of person they wanted to tangle with. Meanwhile, when the detectives visited Rick's parents, his mother fainted at the sight of them, which, in their opinion, was a sign of her son's guilt. The next day, they turned up with shovels, spades, forks, and pickaxes, and then the digging started on the premises. They dug up the entire yard surrounding the house, only to find nothing. The money kept moving from one place to another as fast as the detectives were collecting information about the three suspects. First, it was hidden in a brand-new Prefect car owned by our suspect neighbor. The money was seen by Andrew when he borrowed the car to impress a hot date. Before returning the car, he decided to clean it; and in doing so, he found much of the money hidden in the car. Excitedly, he went to my mom and asked her advice. "Did you put the money in the car?" she sternly asked him. "No," was his soft, submissive reply. "Well, then put it back where you got it from and return the car." Later, the money was moved to the home of one of the suspects' girlfriends and to about ten other places before ending up in the tank of the yard toilet which his family used. The detectives even dug around the same toilet, not realizing how close they were to the money. Now entered my uncle, the jovial one. "Boy, why the hell you went to your mother about the money? You should come to me," smiling as he addressed my brother. Later, the police eventually arrested the three suspects. They were found guilty of fraud and were sentenced to six years' imprisonment.

The wonderful years of my adolescent youth continued with much excitement. As was mentioned, the game of cricket was my heart and soul. My cricketing career started in primary school. I was this little nine-year-old kid in the fourth grade vying for a position in the school team with guys twice my size and three to four years older than me. To make the team, I realized I had to do something extraordinary and spectacular. One day, while on the sideline watching the team practice, a skier ball was played by one of the batsmen out of the reach of the fieldsmen. I darted off like a bullet from a gun, dived forward, and took a remarkable catch to the amazement of the coach. Immediately, he asked me to join the team in the following practice sessions. My batting display startled everyone to the extent that I was included in the team to play in the next competition match. I toured with the team throughout many parts of Guyana, being looked on as a wonder batsman/ fieldsman delight. The ratings of the Smith Church Primary School cricket team shot up because of my batting delight; it was a great feeling. My cricketing ability in primary school helped my scholastic opportunities. High schools were scouting for good players, so I was invited to take an entrance examination at eleven. I started high school at that age, determined to do well academically and in the sport of cricket. With my mom as the driving force for academia, I had to do well in high school. So I listened attentively every morning to the head teacher's comment, "If you fail to prepare, you must prepare to fail."

My cricketing career in high school started with much delight. I had established myself as the number 1 batsman in the team. Getting older, I somewhat developed an air about myself, believing that I can break the school rules without being questioned by anyone. But one day, I had a wide awakening. One of the teachers had done me wrong. "How dare him," I said to myself, marching into the principal's office. After a dialogue with the principal about the incident, he looked at me and said that even though the teacher's action toward me was wrong, he could not have disciplined him. In my inquiry as to why that was so, he remarked, "Because teachers are hard to find, and remember, the teacher knows the work already, but you need to know the work from him. So the teacher is always right barring any criminal act." *Unfair, but logical,* were my thoughts as I left his office.

Being born and raised as a Catholic, my beliefs were always spiritual. So in high school, scripture was one of the subjects I had to pass to graduate. The scripture teacher's son was also in the class. Therefore, he was expected to set an example to the class by doing all homework. But that wasn't the case; he would do the least of the assigned homework. The scripture teacher was short, plump in size, and about forty years of age. She liked to wear a dress with a large buckle head displayed at the back of it. One day, she called on her son to appear in front of the class to explain the parable of the sower from one of the scripture passages. "Miss (all female teachers were addressed as "miss" and the males as "sir" by students), I cannot say it, but I know it," he said to his mom, stuttering. He continued, looking at her dress at the back, "But I do know the parable of the buckle back." The classroom erupted in an uproar as his mom stormed out of the class.

My happy-go-lucky life in high school turned sour in my fourth and final year because of the rivalry between the two main political parties in the country which were racially oriented in their membership. The People's National Congress (PNC) was about 98 percent black with its leader, the late Forbes Burnham being a worldwide highly recognized scholar. The People's Progressive Party (PPP) was made up about the same percentage of East Indians with its leader, the late Dr. Cheddi Jagan, a dentist and a Marxist/

Communist belief–oriented individual with ties to communist Cuba, Russia, and China. The other party, the United Force (UF), was led by the late Peter Deguiar, a wealthy businessman. His party consisted mainly of Portuguese, Amerindians, and mixed-race individuals. The rivalry led to a race riot in 1962 between the East Indians and the blacks. This was one of the darkest moments in Guyana's history. Because of the politics, good neighbors and friends of the opposite race turned on and killed each other. At that time, I witnessed many murders. Being of mixed race and living in the city of Georgetown, predominantly black populated, our family was spared any attacks. The city of Georgetown became a burning inferno; commercial buildings erupted in flames without anyone being seen. We spent many days and nights with our mom, watching the fires to see how close they were getting to our home. Guyana was British Guiana at that time, being ruled by the British government. So they sent in their troops to keep the peace, which resulted, initially, in the random killing of citizens of both races by the British soldiers. During the chaos, I was studying to graduate from high school. This was very difficult because many days, classes were suspended, but prayer gave me the confidence and determination to carry on.

Graduation day eventually came at fifteen years of age, and at the graduation party, I had my first taste of alcohol and the effects of it. Rock, soul music, and close dancing were the "going things" at my age then. When the popular love songs begun to play, it was a mad dash by the guys to get to the girls for a dance. That type of competition never appealed to me. So I just stood by the bar and looked on. One of my classmates asked if I was not dancing. I mentioned that I was hesitant, fearing any of the female classmates would refuse my approach. The classmate said, "Take a drink," offering me a snap glass of rum. Down the hatch the drink went, and within seconds, I was over in the ladies' corner, picking them up one at a time and dancing away. Amazing is this stuff alcohol, giving you courage to do things you're timid about doing. Two months after graduation, I decided to plan my life for the next ten years. Plan A, the number 1 plan, was to become an international cricketer within that ten-year span. Plan B was to become an accountant if plan A failed.

Plan A's first step was to join a reputable cricket club. The Demerara Cricket Club was such a club, being one of the highly rated cricket clubs in Guyana, which produced many Guyanese/West Indian international players. It is interesting to note that geographically, Guyana is the only English-speaking South American country but is culturally Caribbean/West Indian.

Since there were no colleges/universities in Guyana at that time, getting a job became a priority. The jovial one, my uncle worked in a bauxite town about seventy miles from the city where I lived with siblings and my mom. He invited me to join him in the town of Wismar/MacKenzie, a bauxite mining area, to try my luck about getting a job. At sixteen years of age, my adult cricketing career took a jolt. I had to leave home to go somewhere I had no information about, but my hopes were high, and my religious belief helped a lot. Even though the sporting world was my initial choice and the academic world my second, I had to keep up with my schooling. During those adolescent years, I was always all ears and no mouth. Being a very keen listener, I was always told that I had the thoughts and mind-set of a person three times my age. So I set out to check things out about my soon-to-be new environment. To my surprise, there was a recognized cricket club with a Guyanese/West Indian International cricketer as its coach; that was the good part. The bad part was that it was an alcoholic town filled with cheating men on their wives and wives on their husbands and homosexuality, along with an epidemic of social diseases. "Good Lord! What is this?" I asked myself as I pondered on the information, knowing that I was coming from a moral, religious home. My uncle had lived in many of those areas, so no problem for him, being an off-and-on alcoholic himself. But I accepted that that was the adult world and never allowed any peer pressure and other environmental influences overcome me, and I stood firmly by my principles that I learned from home. So with some basic information up my sleeves, I literally set sail with my uncle on a boat, *R. H. Carr*, for the town of Wismar/ MacKenzie. The journey took forever. I arrived tired and weak after a rough twelve-hour boat ride. As a child, I suffered from a gastrointestinal ailment commonly called narah, which was a gastrointestinal ailment developed from jumping from heights and not eating on time. Whenever I got an attack, it would leave me very weak. My mom treated this ailment by placing me on my back and massaging my abdomen. She rarely took her children to the hospital; all her treatments were holistic. During the journey, I had a couple of these attacks, but there was no mom to help me. I felt so alone being on my own at the tender age of sixteen and so far away from home. On arrival in the town, everyone appeared to me as if they were from another planet. Being a bauxite town, there were many white faces on individuals from the dust that bellowed from the plant chimneys. My uncle lived in a room in a hotel-type environment called an inn, and for a couple of years, he resided there. The following week, I tried to get a job with the Bauxite Company but was told that I was too young to work. My uncle then tried to enroll me in the trade school for technicians, and he was told that I was too old for the trade school. So here I was, too young to work and too old for the trade school. Deciding not to waste any time, I concentrated on my other alternative: to obtain membership in the cricket club. One practice session was enough to be selected for team membership, and all first-class games were played in Georgetown, the city. This was great because all traveling expenses were paid by the club and I could be home every weekend. It was during that time I met my first girlfriend, a pretty, light-skinned fifteen-year-old individual of mixed race. It was during my first Christmas away from home and my return home for the holiday season (at that time, I had gotten a job as an insurance salesman selling health-care policies). Her name is Fay. She and some of her friends were visiting my parent's home on Christmas day at the invitation of my older brother. Our meeting was brief, without much exchange of words. Two days later, I returned to MacKenzie via that painstaking boat ride to resume work and then returned home once more to celebrate the arrival of the New Year. While at work, I got a phone call from my brother indicating that he was arranging a date for me with the "pretty thing" I met on Christmas day. At sixteen, that was going to be my first date. I worked until 4:00 p.m. on that Old Year's Day (New Year's Eve). "No way I can take that slow ass boat to be on time," I said to myself. The other alternative was to go by speedboat. Negative thoughts entered mind. *What if the boat overturns? I cannot swim.* Even if one is a good swimmer, few survive the murky water of the famous Demerara River. But this was my first date with a pretty girl from a decent, good home. It was about 5:00 p.m. when I jumped into the speedboat packed with others for my first memorable fast-lane boat ride. "At least I have lots of company in case anything goes wrong," I said to myself. I was also concerned about getting sick from my common "narah" gastrointestinal problem. I said lots of prayers during that ride. It took only two hours to get to the city. I had to have some time to meet my date officially. But I had no suit. I never owned a suit. My brother was waiting for me. "Man, how am I going to go on this date without wearing a suit?" I asked, appealing.

"Don't worry, you will use one of mine." Before I could have fully recovered from the speedy boat ride, another brother excitedly came to the house, asking for me, and left a message with my mom for me to visit him immediately. He just lived a few blocks up the street. I quickly ran over to his home. "I have a date for you for tonight." "But I don't have a suit," I replied. "Don't worry, you can use one of mine," he said in a commanding tone. I asked, "How old is she?" He replied, "About twenty-four." Now here I was with two dates without a suit of my own but both brothers willing to lend me one of their own. That was quite a predicament for me, not wanting to hurt either of their feelings. I pondered to myself about the offers. Knowing what my first brother had to offer—she being innocent and about my age—and having seen her previously compared with the other who was older and whom I haven't seen, I told him how sorry I was because I had to honor the first offer made by our other brother. "Okay, you can still have the suit," was his solemn reply. That was a relief. I quickly hurried back home to find my other brother anxiously waiting on me. He said, "Let's go." Rugged looking from my boat ride, I said, "I have to bathe." "You'll do that later. Come on." We turned up at my date's home, and I met her officially. A guy's appearance to a female is a quality of good character, so she was a bit reluctant but saw a different person when I returned to pick her up to take her to the dance. That night still stands out as the best ever I experienced at an Old Year's Night Dance (New Year's Eve). After that night, we started dating.

The New Year of 1967 was eventful for me. I continued to work as an insurance salesman, trudging up and down the sandy hills and valleys of the town of Wismar, working very hard to make as much money I can make to give to my mom to help with the support of my other smaller siblings, more so my two sisters. I would actually shop for them every two weeks. The salesgirls couldn't believe that the items were for my sisters; they thought they were for some lucky girlfriend of mine.

There were many murders that involved cheating husbands and wives; some of them were insurance policy holders of mine. The Demerara River separated the town of Wismar from that of MacKenzie, but one could have recognized someone else across the river, standing on either bank. Also, the only cinema for both towns was situated on the riverbank of MacKenzie. Many wives used to watch their husbands board the overland boats from Wismar to cross over to MacKenzie for work. At that time, they thought they were safe from being seen by the husband before inviting the other man into their homes, and many times, the husband would return home for something he had forgotten, only to find the other guy in bed with his wife. You can imagine the shock and the rage combined that most times resulted in that individual crossing over that thin line of sanity to lunacy my mom always warned me about. Many times, the victim would die with a knife plunged into his back. Now there was this pretty girl with jet-black hair and the most remarkable body figure, who served meals at the inn where I resided. Almost every adult male was crazy about her, and she felt good about herself rejecting all comers. But I played a psychological game with her. I decided to ignore her presence, and she wanted to know why I was not among the others trying to get a date with her. One day, while she was serving lunch, she left her door key on my lunch table with a note with her address. To be on the safe side, I asked her if she had a boyfriend/husband, and she affirmatively said no. I took up the challenge and appeared at her apartment around 8:00 p.m. that evening. On entering, I noticed how her apartment matched her pretty appearance. I became suspicious. "How can she afford such an apartment with her salary?" I asked myself and then self-replied, "She can't. There has to be a man involve." It was a rainy night, and at about 3:00 in the morning, there was a pounding on the door. I woke her up and asked, "Did you hear that pounding?" Calmly, she said, "Yes." "So who is it?" I nervously asked. "I don't know," she replied in a low tone of voice. *Bam! Bam! Bam! Bam!* the knocking continued. I worriedly said to her, "That knocking sounds like words of 'I live here. Open the blasted door.'" Immediately, I jumped out of the bed and started looking for my clothes. I found and put on every piece of clothing in a jiffy, except for my lumber jacket and shoes, two important items because it was raining. In the meantime, Alma (that was her name) got out of the bed and went to open the door. "A man is in this house," was the harsh, baritone statement by the person at the door. "So what? You always coming at the wrong time," was her aggressive reply. "What the hell is this?" I nervously asked myself as I looked for a way to escape. There was only one door, the front door. At that time, my imagination consumed me with thoughts of being stabbed and running onto the road with a knife stuck in my back, dying, and my mom crying at my funeral as I was just seventeen years of age. "Grab hold of yourself and think constructively," was a sudden thought. As mentioned previously, I liked to use psychology when dealing with other individuals. I decided that it would have been best to approach the individual instead of him finding me in the apartment. So out into the open I went. "Hey, how are you doing?" I calmly asked him. "What are you doing here at this time?" he angrily asked as I approached him to get close enough to restrict any hand movement of his in trying to do me harm, even though he was a massive six feet plus in height and weighing about three hundred pounds of muscle. "Well, I came to sell your girlfriend an insurance health policy," was my steady reply as I worked my way towards= the door to escape. He barked,

"In the dark?" Immediately, I said, "The lights just went out." Suddenly, she bellowed to him, "Get out of here!" Out came a wild swing from him. With her being about one hundred and ten pounds in body weight, the punch lifted her off her feet and sent her flying across the apartment. At that time, while they were fighting, I decided to make good my escape. As I stepped outside with no shoes and no lumberjack to protect me from the rain, I felt a jolting, shivering surge of electricity that moved upward from my feet. "Damn it! If he doesn't kill me this night, the weather will," I said to myself as I darted back into the apartment to see if I can locate both items while she was amazingly fighting back. *Shift, shift, shift* were the sounds coming from where they were rolling on the floor. It then dawned on me that my shoes were under their fighting bodies. I tried rolling their bodies to one side to get my shoes. Then I saw a stare of murder in his eyes. He quickly got up and went into the kitchen, looking for a knife. At that time, I decided it was time to get out of dodge. The loud noise had awakened the neighbors in that area, most appropriately known as the Valley of Tears. The boyfriend came running out of the house, shouting, "Get him! Get him!" Now about ten of his neighbor friends started the chase with him after me. Down the dark road I ran, moving as fast as the lightning that lit up the rainy sky, with a heart rate just as fast and that pounded just as loud as the shattering thunder (as previously mentioned, the Demerara River runs between the two towns of Wismar and MacKenzie, and the only means of transportation was small privately owned riverboats. So I had to cross the river to get to MacKenzie where I lived with my uncle at an inn that was popularly known as the MacKenzie Inn. There were many boat landings where the boats waited for passengers. The boats were busy crossing the river to pick up passengers from a cinema that was located at MacKenzie near the riverbank. Moving fast and with such a high degree of fear for my life, I had placed some distance between me and that threatening mob. As I came to a screeching halt at the landing, the boat was about six feet in the river without passengers; it was going to get passengers who were leaving the cinema. Without any concern for my safety and the fact that I couldn't swim, when I saw those bloodthirsty guys gaining on me, I made a flying leap for the boat, landed on the bow and slid under the seats, and stopped where the boat operator was seated at the back of the boat. Startled, at my acrobatic leap, he said to me, "All you had to do was to wave for me to come back to shore. You didn't have to risk your life, jumping off the landing like that. Oh, by the way, I still have to turn back for more people on the landing." That leap made me speechless, but when he said he had to turn back, I regained my voice. "No! Please don't do that. I will pay for all those guys at the landing," I said to him pleadingly. He chuckled, "Oh, I get it, stranger, eh?" "That's right," was my quick reply. When he safely deposited me on the other side of the shore (MacKenzie), the movie had concluded, and there were swarms of moviegoers waiting to catch the boats to go over to the other shore (Wismar), where I had just miraculously escaped from the devil. Now, without a jacket and barefooted, as I made my way across the sandy shore, I heard voices from some of the moviegoers (who obviously were my insurance policyholders), "Mr. Rillen! Mr. Rillen! Mr. Rillen!" Without looking in the direction of the voices, I quickly made my way to the sidewalk, for, as far as I was concerned, that wasn't my name. On reaching my dwelling quarters, the inn, shivering vigorously from the drenching rain, I immediately drenched my body from head to toes with rubbing alcohol to prevent any fear of pneumonia. Surprisingly, I slept well that night. The next day, that person turned up to work at the inn with my jacket and shoes. I never said another word to her. Here was a woman who decided to get even with her boyfriend because she had seen him with another woman by using another person at the possibly expense of his life.

I had a really tough and abusive boss while working with the insurance company as a salesman. But he was a real spot socially, loved to consume alcohol and party, and wanted all the women he could have laid his hands on, even though he had a wife. He would abuse his employees in the presence of customers when they didn't meet their quota of sales for the week. During my childhood, I always had a nasty temper, and my mom constantly reminded me that there's a thin line between sanity and lunacy. That thought kept me and still does in controlling myself whenever I get angry. Oh! My mom was such a wise person. She was always right most of the time with whatever she used to say to her children. Even now, during my adult life, with her passing away from this life some ten years ago, I always pay attention to what she used to say to me as a child. So one Monday morning (that's the day the boss used to check the books), while checking the books, he angrily blurted out my name and asked, "Where is the f—ing production for last week?" This type of verbal abuse was totally new to me. As growing children, we dared not use any indecent language toward each other. Suddenly, I got quiet. Oh! I get so scared of myself when I get quiet during an argument because that's the time I mentally move toward that thin line my mom used to warn me about. An excited hash female voice bellowed at me and asked what I was trying to do to the boss. I looked at her glaringly and asked, "Trying to do what?" I had the black telephone receiver in my hand and was about to strike the boss in his head with it. She was the secretary. Afterward, I thanked her many times for saving me from committing an obvious serious crime. Realizing, I have a low threshold to cross the sanity line I decided that I have to find a way to prevent myself from getting too angry. I wanted more than anything else to become a career person, be it sports or academia. I could not afford to have problems with the law. In Guyana, one couldn't afford such a flaw in life if you wanted to be a career professional because you had to have that training overseas. To leave the country, one had to have a police clearance which required to be free from any minor offense. Oh, I wish if my mom were around to keep me in line because I was about one hundred miles away from home. I decided not to allow the boss to get angry with me anymore. *How can I do this?* I pondered to myself with much thought. Believing that there is a solution to every problem, I mentally engaged myself in finding one. One day, I went to collect the weekly premium from one of my policyholders who lived by the cemetery and got the idea to use some of the names on the headstones for policyholders and paid out of my pocket for the initial premiums. For months, the deceased were carried on the books, so I had some peace of mind for that time until the auditors from the head office wrote about their upcoming arrival. This sent the boss into a frenzy as it turned out, I was not the only agent that was insuring the dead. The "mother f—" flew from his mouth at everyone when he checked the books, and no one seemed to have an answer about why so many premiums weren't paid. I decided I couldn't risk another encounter with my short-fused temper and cross that thin line, so I made the decision to resign from the job by not turning up to work.

At eighteen years of age, I officially qualified to apply for a job. I went into the employment office of the Demerara Bauxite Company for a clerical job interview. During the interview, the officer indicated that their office didn't have any clerical jobs to offer and the only jobs available were those for laborers. Being a clerk was the stepping-stone for becoming an accountant, which was my academic career passion if my cricketing career didn't materialized. Working at the Bauxite Company was huge in spite of whatever position one held. The main issue was to get in and then work your way up the ladder. So without hesitation, I said to the employment officer, "I will take it." With a surprising look, he said to me, "But you're a high school graduate. Obviously, you wouldn't want this type of job. This job is for the uneducated." I insisted that I will take it and got it. So from a respectable job of an insurance salesman, I made my way downward to be a laborer. During my employment time as an insurance salesman, I made monetary contributions to my mom and sisters. I had to get a job to continue this support. My first day on the job was a laugh for the workers. I was the youngest and the smallest in stature. I was put to work under some giant kilns, rolling tons of bauxite that was being washed with water raining down from about 50 feet above the ground. The foreman asked me to load up a wheelbarrow with spilled bauxite from a hilly area and move it to a location site about twenty yards away. Even though I had never handled a wheelbarrow before, I confidently told myself, "This will be a piece of cake," when I saw how the other workers were wheeling the wheelbarrows around with ease. After loading the wheelbarrow, I grabbed it by the handles in a way to indicate to the other workers that I knew how to handle the job. Two, three, four steps and down the hilly incline I went with the wheelbarrow and the loaded bauxite tumbling and spilling all over me. A fatherly voice from the foreman asked me, "Son, why did you take this job?" The number 3 suddenly appeared in my head. Yes! My probation period was three months. "I am a fast learner. I will do better the next time," I said to him apologetically. My duties as a laborer also included collecting garbage off the streets. This was one of the most demoralizing jobs one can ever have as a young man. While riding on the garbage trailer, I used to hide my head in my arms so that people wouldn't recognized me. My only consolation was the three months' probation. I just needed to get through that period so I could applied for a clerical job to boost my self-esteem. Working around the kilns that dried the bauxite was like living in hell. The heat that radiated from them was around 300 degrees Celsius, and that made my situation worse because I couldn't take a bath for days after being accustomed to bathing twice per day. The misery was unbearable, but in spite of all that, I was always trying to do a good job. That effort of mine was noticed by the kiln operating foreman, who invited me to learn about the kiln operating controls. I did so well so fast that he made arrangements for me to monitor the controls for an indefinite period, with the encouragement of eventually studying to become an engineer. With that offer, the three months' probation didn't look more like a year anymore; and for the first time, I started to appreciate the job I was doing. At the end of my probationary period, I was invited by the kiln foreman to remain in his department as a kiln operator, a very good position. That offer created a conflicting third career option of furthering my education to become an engineer. But I was sticking to my second career option of becoming an accountant. In the meantime, things were going well with my cricketing future. I was traveling to the city in style on the company's luxury speedboat every weekend to play in the cricket competition matches, and I also got the opportunity to see my mom and siblings.

I started my clerical job as an inventory clerk at the conclusion of my probationary period. That was a memorable experience. My foreman was one of those die-hard company men who didn't have much knowledge and carried tales about everyone to the administration and got promoted by years of service. His lack of knowledge for his work, even though he had over thirty years of service, created an envy for any young person with a high school diploma, whom he saw as a challenge to his knowledge of the job. The inventory job was evaluated on a production scale. The boss could have determined how good a worker one was by looking at his worksheet; my worksheet used to be triple the requirement for the day. He was tall and massive looking and felt good when fellow employees show fear in his presence. So one afternoon while on break and chatting with fellow employees, suddenly, I was there alone; the other guys darted off in different directions. They returned five minutes later, and I asked, "Why did you guys run away?" Together, they said in a chorus-like manner, "Because we saw Jim." That was the boss's first name. Then they gave me the details of his attitude toward them. Daringly, I said to them, "Well, when I'm on break and he comes around, I am not going to run." Two days later, the situation repeated itself. He came over to where I was sitting and asked, "Why didn't you run?" My answer was, "I didn't know you're a tiger." He looked at me sternly and walked away with a loud grunt. Afterward, the guys returned and inquired about our confrontation, and they all warned me he would set me up to get me fired. Since I was a kid, I had always shown some interest in the medical field. So when I was asked very nicely by the boss to take inventory of the company's hospital stock, I was glad for the assignment. A couple of weeks into my new assignment, one of the secretaries asked me to visit her home. She was beautiful, with an envious curvaceous body, and she had taken a liking to me. At that time, I got to learn that one of her sisters was epileptic. They were poor like many families and couldn't afford some required medication like supplemental vitamins, which the hospital had lots of on the expired list to be dumped. So I approached the boss and asked him If it was all right to give to the fellow employee a bottle of the expired vitamin for her ailing sister, which he agreed to. That was a big mistake; he saw it as an opportunity to get even with me. The next day, he called me to his desk and accused me of stealing the item. I reminded him of what he said, which he denied but indicated that if the item was returned, he would forget the matter. Growing up in a Christian home and always being reminded by my mom that honesty is the best policy, that situation became confusingly shocking to me. So not realizing he was trying to set me up as the guys had warned me about, I immediately returned the item. He actually jumped for joy when I did return the item. Immediately, he went to the supervisor, who called me into his office and fired me on the spot. Despondent, I started to reminisce about not remaining as a kiln operator before my transfer and that the accounting field may not have been a good career second choice. Now I had to leave the bauxite town and return home.

It was a sad day when I returned home to the city. At nineteen plus years, I had to be dependent on my mom again; worst of all, I could not have helped to support my two sisters who looked forward to the presents of clothing ever so often. Luckily, one of them had recently left for Canada at the invitation of my aunt, my mom's sister. Further to this nightmare, my girlfriend had just given birth to my first son. She lived with her mom and was very understanding about not being able to receive child support, but that didn't make me feel good. I felt that if I were man enough to have a child, I should have been man enough to support that child, job or no job. Fortunately, my mom was preparing to leave for the United States at the invitation of my second-oldest brother who had migrated previously at the invitation of his wife. Three of my siblings left with my mom because they were minors; only my eldest brother and I were left in Guyana. Four years passed without no job, despite countless job interviews. During that time, I concentrated mainly on my first choice career—cricketing; I had only five more years according to my career life plan to make it in the big league.

Competing in the cricketing arena, just like most sports, is tough business. So realizing that my time was short to make it to the big league, I decided that I had to do something extraordinary to gain the eyes of the selectors. For the benefit of the American public, cricket and baseball have some similarities. The pitcher in baseball is the bowler in cricket. The ball has to be pitched at a full length to the batter in baseball, while in cricket, it has to hit the turf before it gets to the batsman (batter). There are mainly three types of bowlers: fast, medium, and slow. With the fast bowler, the ball is delivered to the batsman at a speed of 86–90 miles per hour. Now, with that speed, the wicket keeper (the player behind the stumps/wicket) and whom I was, stands some distance behind to prevent serious injury from the ball. The cricket club I was playing for had such a fast bowler who was playing for the big league, so I decided to do what no other player had done, which was to stand up to the wicket at practice sessions to this fast bowler, much to the amazement of him. My performance was very impressive. I continued with this revolutionary type of wicket keeping, much to the amazement of fellow players. But on the other hand, I was not a sociable person, and that was my "black mark" for being considered for selection.

Two years had passed, and I was still without a job. At that time, my mother had settled in the United States and was able to send me an allowance which I gave to my son's mother to support him. That made me feel much better; the feeling of manhood was amazing whenever I gave her that money.

Family tension had entered our home between my eldest brother and me. Only the two of us were left behind to occupy the house my mother had built when we were kids. He had a good job and was eleven years older than I. One day, he brought home his girlfriend. She was very pretty, but she had her eyes on my mom's house. It didn't take me long to figure her out. However, my brother was blind as a bat where women are concerned and didn't see her for what she was, being a devil in disguise. Her goal was to get me out of the house so she could take over everything. Her initial plan was to cause a rift between my brother and I and then try to convince him to get me out of the house. One evening, after returning from one of my cricket practice sessions, my entire body was aching from muscular stress. I indicated to her that I would go to my girlfriend for a massage. She quickly told me there was no need for that because she could do it. I agreed to her suggestion. During the massage, I realized she wasn't massaging but caressing me. Immediately, I got up and told her that what she did was enough. As soon as I got up, my brother ran up the stairway and came through the doorway; she knew he was around and just wanted him to see us together. Following that incident, I decided to keep away from her, but that was difficult because she prepared our meals. By that time, all other family members and friends had met her and thought she was a very sweet person, but that was her disguise. When I explained the situation to my son's mother, she decided to prepare my meals. I also tried to explain to other family members what a bad person she was, but no one believed me. One day, I said to myself, "Drastic situations require drastic measures," and invited my uncle, the jovial one, and my eldest sister to sit in my room with the door closed so she wouldn't know. No one else was in the house but me. What they witnessed shocked them; she behaved as if she was possessed by the devil. When they opened the door and she saw them, her complexion started to change color like a lizard trying to hide in the bushes. Eventually, she was being exposed for what she is to other family members. Her campaign to get me out of the house intensified. She had my brother hook, line, and sinker to the extent that he complained to my mom in the USA about me making his life miserable. My mom believed him, and she ordered me out of the house, knowing I had no place to go because I had no job. I was never rude to my mom up front, but this was an exception. I told her that I will burn the house down to ashes while they were asleep. She became very concerned and eased off on her demands for me to vacate the house. When they realized trying to persuade my mom wasn't going to work, they concocted another plot. They solicited my father (who was like a stranger to the home because he had another family while still being married to my mom) and my uncle, the jovial one, to a roundtable conference over drinks of alcohol to concoct the best plan to get me out of the house. At the height of their discussion, I turned up and caught them in the discussion. Once again, her complexion changed when she realized I had caught her in the act of her deceit. Feeling guilty, my uncle, well liquored up, jumped to his feet with a bellowing sound and said, "You all think I am a traitor! " With that outburst from him, he now wanted to fight and chase all of them around the house until they took refuge in the bedroom which was separated from the living room by a wall. Up on the chair, he jumped, trying to claw his way over the wall. I managed to calm him down and led him into the street to take him to his house. We walked about one mile when he broke away from me and ran up the street to go back to the scene. I managed to catch up with him about half a mile down the road. It seemed that the exercise had sweat the liquor out of his body because at that time, he calmly went along with me.

Four consecutive years had passed without a job since my return home. At that time, I was twenty-four years old and only had one more year according to my career plan to make it big in the sport of cricket. My frustrations were at that time getting the better part of me after applying in multiple places for a job without any sign of success. One day, I received a letter in the mail from the city constabulary to go in for an interview to become a security guard. That was great news for me. I turned up at the city hall's compound full of confidence to get this long-awaited job, but my confidence was dashed when I saw the trainees being cursed and shouted at by the training officer. Memories flashed back in my head when I worked as an insurance salesman in the city of MacKenzie and nearly fatally injured my boss by an unconscious act for shouting at me. The possibility of this type of anger returning was great; I cannot tolerate anyone shouting at me. I just crossed that thin line my mom always warned me about, and it would have been just a matter of time before that happened if I had taken that job. With a consoling thought, I said to myself, "Prevention is always better than cure," turned around, and went back home.

Guyana was rapidly changing politically. The government had changed and was led by one of Guyana's most brilliant scholars, the late Forbes Burnham who was the prime minister. Socialism was being introduced, and the government had aligned itself with Cuba, Russia, and China at the annoyance of the USA. All foreign investments were being taken over by the government. This required the prime minister to be firm in his decision-making. So firm was he that he became feared by actually all his cabinet ministers. I was now in a do-or-die situation; I had to take the bull by the horns. So I decided to write the prime minister about my situation. (I never liked politics; there is too much treachery and backstabbing in it, and I always wondered how come people repeatedly believe the lies told by these individuals). Never even expecting the prime minister to look at my letter, I was dumbfounded when I received a reply from his office. It was a personal reply from him. Anxiously and full of hope, I turned up at his office for the interview. There were other members of the public waiting to be seen. The guy who sat next to me was so nervous that his legs were making a loud drumbeat sound on the floor. Suddenly, the prime minister shouted, "Desmond!" The late Desmond Hoyte was his minister of finance. Desmond literally flew from his office in response to his name. When the vibrating guy next to me actually saw Desmond in flight trying to get to the prime minister's office, he fell out of his chair. As he scrambled back to his seat, I looked at him and said, "Man, you're a nervous wreck." He responded, "That I am." In his hands he was repeating from a piece of paper notes he made about what he wanted to speak to the prime minister about. When it was his turn, he was out faster from the PM's office than he was in. When he came out of the office, I asked, "How was it?" "I forgot everything I wanted to talk to him about," was his solemn response. Silently, I asked myself, "Why the fear from everyone? He is a person just like me and everyone else." When it was my turn, as I entered his office, I was surprised by his youthful looks. There he sat with a long Cuban cigar bellowing smoke into the air. Suddenly, thoughts came over me in a flash about my mom's counseling while growing up: *Speak the truth and speak it ever, cost it what it will, and you will eventually benefit from it.* All political parties in Guyana have a youth group that advertises the policies of the party and recruits new membership. The Young Socialist Movement (YSM) was the youth group associated with the ruling party, of which the prime minister was the leader. "Are you in the YSM?" was his question, and my response was no. "Why not?" he asked again. I looked at him squarely in the face and said, "I don't like politics." My honesty surprised him, and with a look of admiration, he said to me, "See that you join the YS. Here, take this letter to the minister of agriculture, and he will give you a job." "Thanks, comrade." I responded gleefully and left his office like a flash of lightning.

Seeing that the country was at that time under the official banner of socialism, "comrade" was the official word of address. The medical profession didn't like that form of address because it eliminated the "doctor" salutation. "The long wait is over," I said to myself as I rushed to the Minister of Agriculture Office.

The minister of agriculture was a veterinarian and a graduate of Tuskegee Institute, now Tuskegee University, located in Tuskegee, Alabama. He was tall and dark and had a no-nonsense type of attitude. As I entered his office with the letter in front of me like a six-shooter from the old Western days, I said, "Good morning, comrade. I have a letter from the prime minister for you." With a relaxing posture, he raked back in his chair to read the letter. "We don't have any jobs in the ministry at the moment," was his harsh statement to me coming out from his deep baritone voice. Confidently, knowing that the letter came from the "Cabaka" (that was the prime minister's nickname for being a strong leader), I said to him, "Okay, I will let him know what you said." With bulging eyes and a facial expression of astonishment from my words, he said, "Young man, you can't do that." Why not, you said you don't have any vacancies," was my reply. "We don't. I just have to create one." As mentioned previously, Guyana at that time was nationalizing foreign companies that were literally raping the country of its natural resources for years. Also, about 90 percent of imports, more so food and other agricultural products, were banned from entering the country. As I was growing up, everyone's backyard had fruit trees. That's when I started my cricketing journey. My siblings and I would use the green fruits for balls to play the game. All yards were littered with these fruits when they got ripe and fell to the ground, and at Christmastime, the markets were swamped with imported fruits like apples, grapes, raisins, grapes, prunes, etc., from the United States and England. Some of these fruits were used to make Guyana's special Christmas treat called black cake. Therefore, with Christmas being the most favored holiday season in Guyana, these imported items were always associated with that season. So the ban was placed to allow the government to create those special ingredients to make the beloved black cake from the local fruits that were squandered, but change is hard to accept. Most of the population now thought that Forbes Burnham, the prime minister, was such a bad person to take away their Christmas delight with the ban. So the Ministry of Agriculture was given the responsibility of creating a recipe for black cake using the local fruits. So while sitting in the Minister of Agriculture office and waiting for my job placement, he picked up the phone and called his permanent secretary (second in command) who was directing operations in the initial stages of creating the factory and said, "I am sending a young man over to your office for a job placement." His reply probably was negative because I heard the minister said, "Find one!" Then he looked up at me and said, "You're all set." I hurriedly made my way over to the factory and was assigned the position of purchasing clerk. I thought that this was great because this position was the stepping-stone to my planned (plan B) accountancy career. My job involved purchasing material ingredients for the factory and accounting for money spent. The process involved me taking advance cash from the accounting division of the Ministry of Agriculture to make purchases and clearing the advance with the receipts from the purchases and refunding the difference. (I was approaching twenty-four years of age and had only one year remaining to make it big in my cricketing career bid as planned, but I doubted that this would have materialized according to the situation at that time.

So I decided to concentrate on my academic plan B career in the field of accountancy).

As soon as I got the job, I moved out from my mom's house, left my brother and his wife (he had recently got married), and went on my own. My mom revisited Guyana to sponsor my brother to migrate to the USA along with his wife. During her visit, she was totally taken in by the charm of my brother's wife to further disbelieve what I had said about her. So far, my mom had sponsored all her children to the United States, except for the two of us. During her visit, I had asked her to sponsor me, but she refused, being convinced by my brother that she shouldn't. So out of my mother's nine children, I was the only one left behind. I was never so hurt. I was always tough and could have never seen myself crying under any situation, but that day, the tears and hurt were overwhelming. My consolation was "One day, old lady (as previously mentioned we had always referred to my mom in that way), you will find out what an evil person your daughter-in-law is." "So said, so done," as relayed by my other siblings, she made my mom's life a living hell, to the extent that she had to move out of her apartment where she invited them to live in with her until they had gotten on their feet financially.

Six months had passed, and I was really enjoying my job. Besides working in the field of my intended career, I was being part of a historic event in the making of Guyana's famous fruit cake with locally grown fruits. Then on one bright and sunny day, my birthday, with high spirits as usual when I turned up for work, my career aspirations took a twist. There on my desk was a letter from the head office that notified me of my transfer to the veterinary division. Of course, I was very reluctant to leave the job, so reluctant that I dodged the transfer for a couple of weeks, trying to find out the reason for it. With the government, there are two reasons for a transfer; you're either a good worker or a bad one. Being the latter would not have been good for my future aspirations. On the other hand, I knew I was a good worker, but I was still worried about the reason for the transfer. Eventually, I turned up at the veterinary division after a stern warning from the head office. It so happened that the administration had observed me to be a strong, no-nonsense person and the new position required such a person. I reported to the chief veterinary officer, who made me aware of my duties as a veterinary pharmaceutical clerk. It was a challenging job; the pharmaceutical division was a mess. There was no accountability for drugs used by the veterinarians who used their position to demand the drugs from the previous clerks without the required requisitioning. My job was to reorganize everything and bring order to the division. On my first day at work, the senior veterinarian came barging into the room and was packing his bag with the drugs when a loud shout came from the chief veterinary officer, "Doctor, what the hell do you think you're doing? Don't you see the clerk is on duty?" With that shout, the doctor dropped all the drugs like a child who was caught with his hand in the candy jar. Now remember that thin line between sanity and lunacy I spoke of when someone reaches that threshold of tolerance with anger? That flashed into my mind when I saw how that veterinarian reacted when he was shouted at by the boss. Once again, I said to myself, "I do hope this guy never shouts at me because I don't know how I will react." Additionally, racism was a major problem in Guyana between races, which consisted of East Indians (49 percent), Africans/black people (35 percent), Amerindians (7 percent), mixed race (7 percent), and Portuguese (2 percent). The government was either Indian or black, and this led to rivalry between the two groups. People of light color had most of the advantages, while people of darker color had the least advantages; all of these resulted because of slavery. Even though the government was predominantly black, this type of color submission or inferiority complex, along with poor self-esteem, still existed in many individuals. So being Portuguese, the boss, the chief veterinary officer, was feared by actually all the staff that were mainly black. I decided to observe the other staff (veterinarians, technicians, the secretary, and clerks) to see their interactions with the boss. When he wanted anything done, he used to come out of this office, screaming and shouting at the staff, and they, in return, would be scrambling and bumping into each other. "This, I will not tolerate," I said to myself as I pondered the situation. So I approached his secretary, whom the guys loved to hang around with, and asked her opinion of his attitude, and at the same time, I enlightened her about myself, indicating that I will do everything I can where the job is concerned to avoid a situation of him raising his voice at me because she said he couldn't help it.

The inevitable eventually happened. After about six months into the job, the boss sent one of his patients' owner to me for a particular shampoo to treat a skin infection the pet was having that was making his life miserable. I checked my inventory book, which indicated zero balance from the retailed container. The next day, I took off on a week's leave, and the boss's veterinary assistant filled in for me during my absence. The boss asked him to order the shampoo that I reported was out of stock, but he reported that the shampoo was in stock. Since it was a retailed item, some was left in the bottle. However, the boss thought that for some reason, I didn't want sell his client the shampoo. On my return, I was asked to report immediately to the boss's office. Inside his office was his secretary typing some personal work for him. He confronted me about my report on the nonavailability of the shampoo. Before I could start explaining the situation, he shouted at me. Immediately, I shouted back at him. His face turned pink, either with the shock of surprise or respect because no one had responded to him like that before. After a long pause, he calmly said to me, "Mr. Rillen I didn't mean anything personal. I have a high amount of adrenaline that makes me angry." My response was firm, "Doctor, I have a high level of adrenaline too, and I don't like anyone to shout at me." When the secretary left his office, she said to me, "No one has never spoken to him like that before," and feared that he may have recommended my dismissal. On the contrary, he acquired a high degree of respect for me because I was doing a very good job with the previously chaotic pharmaceutical division, and he realized that I was a no-nonsense type of person. It is interesting to note that one does not have to kiss ass to get by. Just know and do your work efficiently; even though sometimes "figure heads" (persons with least knowledge of their work) are promoted to positions of authority because of their ignorance and they wouldn't be a threat to the administration. I have seen ass-kissers get promoted, but it does not last for any length of time because no boss respects such a person; they just love being kissed up to. I have always used a senior veterinary assistant as an example, who would always run to the boss with bad reports about his colleagues. The boss loved the reports because he became knowledgeable about the whereabouts of his technicians when they were in the field, but he never trusted the senior veterinary assistant. Further, those same technicians he reported on were being selected by the boss to receive additional training overseas, but not him. So one day, he became frustrated, went to the boss, and asked why he wasn't being chosen for any of the overseas training, and the boss mentioned to him that he cannot be trusted. That was the end of the news-carrying exercise by that particular employee.

The boss's tantrums with the staff got worse as time went by, and I used that situation to my advantage, knowing that everyone, except yours truly, was scared of him. Being the pharmaceutical purchasing clerk, I was tasked to requisition drugs for the veterinary division, which had to be ordered from overseas, and this order had to be placed by other clerks. So whenever they were late with placing the order, I used to mention to whomever was supposed to place the order that a complaint would be made to the boss about the matter at hand. Whenever that was said, I used to get immediate action. Further, many times when I wanted to see the boss, his secretary used to say to me, "Mr. Rillen, the boss is in a bad mood, I don't think you should see him." At that time, I used to remind her about her presence in his office; when he shouted at me, I shouted back at him. So whenever I received that warning from her and entered his office, I used to make a face as if someone had angered me. When he saw that, his facial expression would change, and then we would have a soft and cordial conversation.

The final curtain closed on my plan B career of being an accountant when one day, I received a call from the head office to report to the accounting division. There, I saw some police officers awaiting my arrival. Nervously, I asked myself, "What do they want from me?" I reported to the accountant and was told that the police was investigating a fraud involving me. "Fraud! What the hell are you talking about?" I asked him. He mentioned that I didn't clear an advance which I took from the accounting division to purchase materials while I was with the Special Projects Department before my transfer. At that time, I worshipped my mom with thoughts of gratitude for instilling in me not to trust anyone, more so your so-called friends and/or those close to you. So I used to keep copies of all records related to government affairs. Every advance I took from the head office to make purchases, I had copies of receipts from the head office which I had placed in a folder and had given to my children's mother for safekeeping. With that assurance, I approached the police officer in charge of the investigation and asked for about half an hour to go and get the folder. On my return, I presented the documents to the police, and they, in turn, arrested the accountant. Later, I was told that my case of suspected fraud wasn't the first one involving the accountant. Previously, he had other clerks within his department arrested and fired and probably jailed for fraud because they had no hard proof of their innocence, for he was the one that committed the fraud and blamed it on his clerks. From that experience, I concluded that if the career of accountancy involved fraud and setting people up to make oneself look good, I didn't want any part of it. So I decided to look at veterinary medicine as an alternative third option career.

Since my adolescent years, I had found myself to be very scornful of my surroundings. Everything had to be clean, and even though clean, it seemed to be never clean. At that time, each of the siblings had assigned house chores. One of my chores was washing the dirty kitchenwares. While the glassware shined with cleanliness, to me, their appearances were still dirty, so I would force my hand with the washing sponge into the drinking glass to make it cleaner. Many times, the glass would break and give me cuts all over my right hand. I would also find myself spitting continuously if anything appeared dirty. With these idiosyncrasies, I had my reservations about pursuing a career in veterinary medicine. However, my planned career options had been exhausted, and I was getting older. I only had a career plan A and B, no plan C. Therefore, I told myself, "I have to overcome these peculiarities about myself."

A senior veterinarian, an employee of the veterinary division, who was or thought he was a flamboyant, ladies' man type of veterinarian, was looking for an assistant to work with him at his after-hours clinic. I approached him about the position, and he decided to give me the job. His clinic was located in a basement-type apartment, with the entrance facing the street. On my first afternoon on the job, as I approached the clinic from the street, I saw him with his face close to a gangrenous leg of a pet dog, and he was holding a scalpel blade and dissecting away at the intended amputation of the leg. As I got closer, the smell had me reeling with continuous uncontrollable vomiting. On hearing my loud retching, he looked up and said to me with a smile on his face, "Come on in. You'll get over it." Slowly, I made my way into the clinic, and amazingly, the vomiting stopped, enabling me to assist him with the amputation.

In 1975, working for about three years with the veterinary division and for about a year with that senior veterinarian in a clinical, practical environment, I was confident that I had absorb enough technical information, interacting with the veterinarians and technicians, to decide that it was time for a promotion. On one bright and sunny day, I thought the atmosphere was right to approach the boss about the promotion. Boldly, I walked into his office and asked to be promoted to the position of livestock assistant (a field position). He leaned back into his chair, and I said to myself, "He's reflecting on our first encounter when he shouted at me and I shouted back at him." But to my surprise, he enlightened me about a new semi-veterinary school that was about to be opened in my country to accommodate students from all over the Caribbean and encouraged me to apply for a government scholarship. I applied and was granted a government scholarship to attend the Regional Educational Programme for

Animal Health Assistants. The school employed only veterinarians who came from many foreign countries to lecture to students. It was an intensive two-year program. The administration wanted the school to be a success, so they rammed down our throats a four-year veterinary program in two years. Being out of high school for almost twelve years, the going was tough, but I held my own. The discipline that was instilled in me as a child by my mom and my distrust for individuals served me well. In the second year of the program, there was an outbreak of anthrax among a herd of cattle in close proximity to the school's compound. As part of the training, samples from livestock were collected and brought to a laboratory to be used for microbiological analysis. I handled the initial samples from the herd which were plated and incubated for growth of bacterial organisms. After twenty-four hours of incubation, there was massive growth on the biological plate. The color, smell, and growth were used to determine what type the organism/s is/are before microscopic evaluation. Being the diligent student that I was, I smelt the plate. Immediately, I felt the rush of microbes up my nostrils. "What the hell was that?" I asked myself. Forthwith, I reported to the veterinarian who was from India and taught the course. During a microscopic evaluation of the organism, he solemnly looked at me and mentioned that organism was anthrax. (Anthrax can be a fatal disease if not treated early.) I nervously asked the veterinarian if he was sure about what he had seen. Authoritatively, he said, "I am quite sure. I have seen it many times in my country." "Good Lord, what is this?" I said to myself as I appealed to the almighty for guidance. Whenever I am in any kind of trouble, I always seek help from the Almighty God. Immediately, I reported the matter to the veterinarian in charge of the program, who was a Guyanese trained in Canada. He looked at the slide and smilingly said with a frown on his face, "This is not anthrax." I asked him if he had seen anthrax before. His reply was negative, but he indicated that we haven't had an outbreak since the early thirties and we don't want to cause a panic in the community. I said to him that as far as I was concerned, I believed the other doctor because he has had the experience of seeing and working with the disease. With that statement to him, I immediately left the school compound, traveled to the agriculture office. and notified my former boss, the chief veterinary officer, about the matter. At that time, he mentioned that he'll have to get a report from the veterinarian I had questioned about his knowledge of the disease. Abruptly, I left his office, concluding that by the time they go through all the red tape, I would most likely come down with the disease. My previous position as a pharmaceutical clerk had given me the knowledge of how to treat the disease, so I immediately started a three-week course of antibiotics. Two months later, it was declared that there was an outbreak of anthrax.

In 1977, I graduated with the diploma in Animal Health And Veterinary Public Health. Almost immediately, my new position as veterinary assistant exposed me to fieldwork. At that time, I decided to work as hard as I can to create a good impression with my superiors so as to earn another scholarship to complete my career goal of becoming a veterinarian. Ironically, I was assigned to work with that doubting veterinarian about the anthrax outbreak. Whenever we went out into the field, most of which became very slush like when the rain fell, he would stand on dry ground and make me do all the muddy legwork of restraining the livestock, more so pigs. Farmers in Guyana always appreciate interest shown by government livestock officers in their welfare, and whomever made their animals better, they respected him as the veterinarian, whether he's is the vet or the assistant.

One bright and sunny afternoon saw a farmer in one hell of a mighty rush. He was skipping stairs with panting breath as he got to the secretary's desk. "I want to see the doctor. I have an emergency," he said to the secretary as he took deep breaths. At that time, the doubting veterinarian I worked with came out of his office and approached the secretary, who then enlightened the farmer that he was the veterinarian he was supposed to see. Alarmingly, the farmer said he is not the doctor, he is the assistant. Just as he had finished saying those words, I appeared on the scene, and when he saw me, he alarmingly said to the secretary, "This is the doctor." Then he beckoned me to his side and explained the emergency, much to the shocking amazement of the doubting veterinarian. Livestock veterinarians in Guyana have always had a difficult time dealing with farmers because of the fact that 100 percent are trained overseas, mainly in the United States and England. They don't seem to know how to readjust to the demands of the environment and seem to place themselves above farmers and pet owners. So initially, farmers are resistant to the advice of veterinarians because most of their problems are management oriented and most veterinarians have little knowledge of management practices. They also try to conceal this deficiency by evading management issues and try to enforce therapeutic practices. Many veterinarians, like most medical doctors seem to honor themselves by being direct with their advice like "This is the problem" (meaning, that whatever the problem is, that is the only one), and forget to use words like "Most likely, this is the problem," indicating that there can be another. One senior veterinarian I worked with found this out the hard way. He responded to an emergency request from a farmer about his pregnant cow. After examination of the animal, he told the farmer that the cow would not give birth for another month. The next day, the farmer angrily came looking for the veterinarian; the cow had given birth about five hours after he left the farm. This was very embarrassing for the veterinarian because the farmer demanded of him not to visit his farm again.

I continued to apply myself diligently in the field of veterinary medicine as a veterinary assistant during my four years' contract with the government. So much was my hard work that my ability outshone those of the veterinarians. Farmers became so impressed with my work that they always referred to me as their veterinarian, with salutation to me as "doc." Even though flattering, I never took anything for granted. Many of them would ask me, "Doc, how come when you do a C-section (cesarean) on my cows, they survive, and when the other veterinarians do them, they don't survive?" A farmer of Indian decent repeatedly said to me, "Doc, you are a special type of person. You have to have *graa* (meaning some type of supernatural power). Every time my cows are sick for days, I always know when you're coming because they would just get up and walk away." Then there were times my wife told me when farmers and pet owners used to assemble in front of my premises and argue about whom I should go with first to look at his animal. This type of attention made me realized how important my services were to the veterinary public, but all I wanted to do was a good job. Without realizing it, my work was also noticed by the chief veterinary officer, who would send me on assignments that were meant for the veterinarians. So much was his confidence in me that I was given the task on many occasions to organize the National Veterinary Exhibition, a task for someone with major academic qualifications.

Bribery and corruption spare no government officer in terms of exposure. Few go clean, but most accept the bribery because the monetary payback was great. But I am proud to say that I have always had a clean slate. I have always known that through prayer, honesty was always the best policy. Further, my mom's warnings about accepting the bad things in life always reveal themselves at some time or the other. "Anything bad that you do in life leaves a scar that never goes away," she would always warn while I was growing up. Additionally, being very proverbial, she always warned, "Moonlight runs until daylight catches up with it," meaning that anyone can do anything for only a period of time until he/she is eventually caught doing such wrong. She was such a wise woman, even though she left school in the third grade. (Now I am taking a pause in my writings because I am becoming very emotional thinking about the good things she has done for me and my other siblings by herself without any particular help from my father. God bless and rest her soul.) With her words that always kept ringing in my ears, I was always on the lookout for trouble.

In my second year of being a veterinary assistant, I was summoned to the office of the chief veterinary officer, who immediately assigned me to the abattoir (slaughterhouse for animals) to conduct veterinary duties. These duties involved checking livestock (mainly cattle) to qualify them for slaughter. In the qualifying process, animals had to be nonproductive. Only male calves and culled cows could have been slaughtered; female calves and productive cows were spared to boost the government's program of increasing the cattle industry. Qualifying for slaughter also involved the police department. The only duty of the police officer was to verify the brand on the animals to be legitimate. Therefore, passing an animal for slaughter required the veterinary division, which I represented and the police department. On many occasions, the police officer would pass animals without my examination. On investigation, I found that those were rustled animals, and the police officer was working for the rustlers. The chief rustler was always on sight at the abattoir to be seen by everyone to avoid suspicion. The stolen animals were brought to the abattoir late in the afternoon when I wasn't around and slaughtered during the night. When this was known, I decided to make a random visit late one afternoon and caught them in the act of illegal slaughter. Knowing the police officer was involved, I decided to go to the police headquarters to make a report to the commissioner of police, but one of the employees at the abattoir counseled me not to do so because the police officer was the nephew of the commissioner. On the other hand, I figured that the commissioner most likely didn't know about the illegal activities of his nephew, so I proceeded to the police headquarters. On my arrival, I barged into the commissioner's office and was confronted by his secretary who indicated that I had to make an appointment, but I was in no mood for protocol. I left her desk and quickly pushed open the door to his office, identified myself, and proceeded with my complaint, including that I was informed the police officer was his nephew. "I was told that you are the one that is doing what you're accusing my nephew of doing," he blurted out at me (at that moment, one of my mother's teachings came right at me, "do nothing fear nothing."). Good, so investigate both of us," was my reply. I had stopped him in his tracks; he never expected that type of reply from me. "Well, on second thought, that will be conflict of interest. I will assign the duty to one of my senior officers," was his reply. The senior officer whom he assigned to the investigation was the crime chief who was also involved in criminal activities. So he met me at the abattoir to initiate the investigation. Noticeable was the convenient absence of the police officer. Two hours into the supposed investigation, the secretary quickly called me to her desk and told me to look out of the window near her desk. To my amazement, two of the abattoir workers who also worked for the cattle rustler were loading half sizes of beef carcasses into the police investigator's truck. "This is bigger than you think, Doc (everyone referred to me by that name). You're wasting your time and putting your life in danger," was the secretary's comment. But because of my strong religious belief, I felt that some guardian angel was always looking over me and no one can cause me harm. So in spite of concerned warnings from fellow workers, I continued trying to expose the individuals. During the investigation, the deputy chief inspector at the abattoir decided to help me expose those involved with the rustling at the abattoir because the chief inspector was also involved up to his neck. The situation became one of much concern for the chief rustler, who was always seen at the abattoir. That was his cover. So he decided to use bribery to keep me quiet, and I decided to play his type of game. An amount of $1000 was offered by one of his employees. I told him that wasn't enough, then $2000, still not enough, and at five $5000, the employee said to me, "The boss wants to know what is your game." Angrily, I said to him, "Tell your boss even if he offers ten million dollars, it still wouldn't be enough. In plain English, tell him I cannot be bought." That made his boss raving mad; no one had refused his bribery before I came on the scene. He commented, "I will get rid of his little ass one way or the other." I must say that comment made me somewhat fearful, and at that time, I realized that my faith was somewhat weakened/compromised. So I prayed for more strength in my belief of the Almighty. Amazingly, the fear was gone, but I remained careful and started to construct a strategy to counter his treats. In countries like Haiti, Suriname, Guyana, etc., many people are superstitious, mostly those in Haiti and Suriname. Suriname is one of three countries that borders Guyana, and there are lots of migration between the two countries. My father migrated to Guyana, formerly British Guiana, from Suriname, formerly Dutch Guiana. The Dutch somewhat equals Haitians with superstitious intensity. So I decided to use that belief to my advantage, even though I don't have much belief in it. During one of his threats to me, I told him of my heritage, and if he continues to threaten me, I will light three candles, white, black, and yellow, and place them where he can see them, and by morning, he wouldn't be able to walk. Those words ended the verbal threats, but I knew he was still trying to do me harm. So one busy day at the abattoir, while I was on the floor inspecting the cattle presented for slaughter, I got a loud excited call from the clerk whose office was about twenty feet above the floor to go immediately to his office. I ran up the stairway and excitedly asked, "What's wrong?" "Those guys were trying to set you up for a stabbing. Please leave the abattoir and go home." Instead of becoming fearful, I got mad, went back on the floor, and confronted the suspects who denied everything. Now I had to find a new strategy to offset further attempts on my life.

The political turmoil in the country had its impact on everyone's life. The rivalry between blacks and East Indians continued from the riots of 1963. The ruling party was black, and the opposition was Indian. The cattle rustler was Indian, along with most of his employees. The blacks in his employ only got work from him when it was too much for his Indian employees. I am of mixed race, so my appearance wasn't full for either side, and I used that to my advantage. The suspected rustled cattle I held over for verification used to be taken out of their pens and slaughtered at a nearby riverside after hours. This was threatening to the public health of the population because many well-fleshed cattle were infected with tuberculosis, and illegal slaughter meant that those animals could not have been inspected before the meat was sold to the public. Commonly, an animal infected with the disease is very thin with continuous coughing; and many times, neither of these symptoms was present. Therefore, to reduce the threat to the public, I had to be lenient with my actions so at least the animals could be slaughtered within the abattoir and the meat inspected. To get some of the rustler's henchmen, who were mainly black, on my side, I struck a deal with the rustler. All rejected animals should have been allowed to be slaughtered conditionally. The condition was that all work had to be given to the blacks. This move resulted in the blacks looking on me as their savior because most of them, even though with a criminal history, had families to support and they needed the work. These same workers were the persons being used by the rustler to threaten my life. Now I gained some ground against the rustler; I had gained the trust of some of his employees and, therefore, some protection. When he realized that the threats weren't scaring me, he decided to set me up to disgrace me within my job. Only healthy male and old animals (male and female) qualify for slaughter, as well as inbred animals and/or runts. Female calves, heifers, and young cows didn't qualify for slaughter because the government was trying to boost the livestock population. The boss man rustler would present female calves (young animals) for slaughter and claim that they were old animals, but on examination, they were determined to be young female calves and rejected for slaughter. Bent on trying to disgrace me with my job, on a particular day, he went to the office of the chief veterinary officer and brought him to the abattoir to examine the young female calves I rejected, claiming they were old animals (some old animals sometimes appear young if they are runts or inbred). To tell the difference, one has to be experienced with teeth examination of those animals. On arrival at the abattoir, I asked the chief veterinary officer why he came to the abattoir. He mentioned he got a complaint about me where the aging of rejected animals was concerned. I invited him to check the animals. After checking the animals, he turned to the boss man rustler and said that I was right and totally in charge of all proceedings. Those words made him mad as hell. He then indicated to me that he would still try to do everything to have me removed from the abattoir.

The boss man realized that I was a thorn in his flesh while being in charge of the veterinary proceedings at the abattoir. One sunny afternoon, I heard a big commotion on the floor of the abattoir; the boss man rustler, with a couple of his henchmen, came up and said, "Mr. Law and Order, let's see how you handle this one." The late president of Guyana and his late wife were into the cattle and buffalo business, and some of the workers had brought in some of their animals for slaughter without any form of identification. The boss man rustler saw this situation as a means to resort to his old ways of breaking the law because he felt I couldn't enforce them with the president's animals. I asked the handlers, "Why these animals don't carry a brand?" The reply was that no one never asked for any form of identification. All eyes were now on me as I made my way to the office to call the president. On contact with his office, the late first lady answered the phone. I identified myself and asked for verification of the animals sent in to be slaughtered from her farm. She indicated that no one ever asked for those requirements. "Comrade, you know how tense the political environment is at the abattoir, and with me enforcing the rules for everyone, I am being placed in a compromising position if I allow your animals to pass for slaughter," was my explanation. "But I don't like branding animals. I think it's cruel," she replied. I then advised her that any form of identification would work besides branding. We then agreed to apply numbered tags around the neck of each animal. Everyone who had gathered around me stood in amazement because I had allowed them to listen in on the conversation. Now I had the entire situation under control, and the boss man rustler started to back off from trying to harm me, but his rustling activities continued, involving many high-profile government officers, including senior police officers. The same senior police officer that the commissioner of police had assigned the duties of investigating the corruption at the abattoir was the biggest crook of all. He was so outright with his behavior that he asked me to monitor his farm if there were any health problems among the animals. He had his farm in an isolated area up the Demerara River, one of the major rivers in Guyana. My first visit to his farm was interesting; he had about two hundred head of cattle. On close examination, I observed all animals within view had different brands. I asked him how come his animals had different brands. He replied, "You really don't want to know." I took that as a warning and never brought the subject up again. In the meantime, he was conducting his so-called investigation of corruption at the abattoir and receiving large portions of meat from the boss man rustler.

My bold and direct approach to the president's wife about the law for the slaughtering of animals seemed to have resonated well with her. She had chosen me instead of any of the veterinarians on staff to consult with about the welfare of her farm animals (cattle and buffalo). Her confidence grew in me when, at one of the agricultural exhibitions, I was able to predict the calving of one of her buffaloes which was taken to the exhibition site on the opening day for that purpose. This situation boosted the chief veterinary officer's confidence in me a great deal to the extent that I was the first person called on to handle any major veterinary problem occurring within the country, much to the annoyance of the veterinarians.

In 1977, there was a foot and mouth disease outbreak in the rural Rupununi region of Guyana. This is the main savanna land of Guyana (grassland without any roads), mainly populated with cattle, that stretches to the border with Brazil. So to effectively control the spread of the disease, I was called on to go into that area. On arrival, I was showered with many complaints about the local veterinarian appointed by the Ministry of Agriculture, who had set himself up as kingpin of the area, driving around with the government's Land Rover vehicle and spreading the disease from farm to farm. Remember that I was a veterinary assistant at that time, but my previous training was on the level of that of a veterinarian, so even though that was the case and the veterinarian was my senior, I was given the authority to supersede his seniority. So I approached him, and without making him aware of my authority, I requested of him to bring me up-to-date with the situation, which he didn't had a clue of because I observed from the information he had given me that he didn't know much about disease control. We set out to go out into the field to set up tents to control movement of the cattle. At the first site, which was in the middle of nowhere, he decided to get back into the vehicle and told the driver to take him back to the hotel which was about fifty miles away. I confronted him, letting him know that we were supposed to do the work together. This he refused, and my response to him was the command "Move over," referring to the seat in the vehicle. "If you're going back to the hotel, I am doing likewise," were the following words from me. Back at the hotel, I radioed the chief veterinary officer (CVO) and brought him up-to-date with the situation. The next day, the CVO arrived and instructed the veterinarian to do the fieldwork, but without my presence. Besides the movement of cattle, the movement of by-products were also prohibited, and it was disclosed that senior police and government officers were moving these items out of the area, thereby increasing the risk of spreading the disease out of the area. I was asked to manage the airport to prevent any by-products from leaving. The next day, two senior police and government officers arrived at the airport with lovely ornaments made from the long horns of cows. As they approached the area to the tarmac of the plane, I reminded them that they could not leave with their souvenirs. One of them asked, "Do you know who I am?" "I don't care," was my response. "You will have to leave those items behind." I continued, "Or do you want me to notify the president?" With those words from me, they didn't utter another word as they gently placed the items down at my feet and boarded the plane.

In spite of all the plans we make for the future when we're young, sickness is something many of us don't envisage. While sharing an apartment with some friends (two females and one male who was the boyfriend of one of the females) from my workplace, the boyfriend believed that I was sleeping with his girlfriend because she used to complain to me about the beatings she received from him. One morning, while stepping out of the door of my room, I felt something stuck at the bottom of the greater toe (big toe) of my left foot. At first, I didn't feel much concern for the injury. But after a couple of days, a sore erupted at the side of the toe. Nothing could heal the lesion; the doctors were puzzled, seeing nothing was helping. I then realized that the boyfriend had most likely placed something poisonous on the floor for me to walk on. In spite of the injury, I kept on working. My belief that the boyfriend was responsible got stronger when I was told by the other female roommate that whatever I tried, my foot would never heal.

A sudden string of deaths among the government's horses in another rural area of Guyana, the northwest region, resulted in another assignment for me. At that time, that assignment was near the famous Jim Jones commune, near the Venezuela border with Guyana. While I was taking blood samples from the horses, one of them stepped on my injured toe. The next morning, the foot got worse, and I had to be hospitalized. While hospitalized, a middle-aged man who was found in the densely wooded forest was admitted suffering from hypothermia and dehydration. He had escaped from Jim Jones Peoples Temple, the religious cult that committed murder/suicide. In those areas of Guyana, the dispensers (pharmacists) run the hospitals because there are no doctors on staff. After examining my toe, the pharmacist decided to extract the toenail. The next morning, there were multiple fistulas (channel-like lesions with fluid) on the instep of my foot. This was really bad; the pharmacist had no clue about the problem. The next day, I was flown to the city for medical treatment. When I visited the doctor, he too had no clue about the problem but wanted to give me an injection of penicillin. I was hesitant after recollecting about the many persons I had heard of who had died almost immediately from anaphylactic shock after receiving an injection of penicillin. I opted for the capsules instead and went home. After one week of taking the capsules, my older brother paid me a visit. When he saw me, he blurted out, "What the hell happened to you!?" Nervously, I asked, "What do you mean?" His next question was, "Have you looked at yourself in the mirror?" I ran back to the bedroom, picked up the mirror, and was shocked at the look of my face, which was about three times its normal size. This was an anaphylactic reaction to the ampicillin I was taking. I then praised the good Lord above for refusing the injection form of the drug because if that was given, I would have dropped dead. In spite of taking the medication, my foot got worse; the vesicles that formed on my instep ruptured, and the fluid was pouring out with a foul smell. After seeing my condition, my brother immediately took me to the hospital. It was a private Catholic hospital, and the doctors there also didn't have a clue about the infection which had caused my footpad to completely peel off. After two days in the hospital, I received the nickname "stink foot" from the nurses. I heard them arguing among themselves every morning as to whom should have changed my bandage because of the smell. Fear got the better part of me when I saw the hospital surgeon appeared at my bedside. I said to myself, "Surgeon spells amputation." The next day, I asked to see the priest. When he came, I asked him to help me pray for a cure of my foot because this was the same leg I nearly lost when I got it broken as a kid. We prayed together, and amazingly, the fear vanished from my mind, and then I started thinking clearly. I had received the Merck manual, which I referred to as the bible of veterinary medicine during my training. During one of her visits, I asked my intended wife, who was the mother of my two small children, to bring the book for me to research for a cure for the infection. Not knowing where to start looking for the information in this thick manual, I decided just to open it randomly, and there the information was right in front of my eyes. Animals, many times, do have the same infection. It was a combination of a fungus, staphylococcus/ streptococcus bacterial infection. In the meantime, the fluid was pouring out of my foot as if one had opened a tap of water.

The treatment for the infection consisted of a steroid and an antifungal/bacterial solution. On one of her visits, I had asked a former girlfriend to see if she could have purchased the medication from a drugstore. She only got the steroidal cream. The problem was to get someone to apply it to my foot. So I decided to befriend one of the nurses, promising her to fill the void her previous boyfriend had left her with that made her somewhat miserable. She applied the cream, and to my amazement, the next morning, the bandage was dried; the fluid had stopped as if one had turned off a tap of running water. The word got around in the hospital about my improvement. The doctors knew they didn't contribute to my sudden improvement. So they raided my cupboard that night while I was asleep and found the cream. The next day, they advised me to discharge myself, seeing that I didn't want to accept their treatment. This I gladly accepted, and the next day, I was out of the hospital.

I turned out to work with my foot strapped to the top of my shoes. But there was one problem: my foot was numb. The pad of my foot had completely peeled off and was raw. No feelings meant that there was no life in the tissue. Amazingly, I had no fear. The same friend who had gotten the cream to stop the fluid flow from my foot mentioned that she could make an appointment with an English dermatologist friend of hers who was in charge of the leprosy asylum in Guyana. Previously, the public hospital in Guyana had made an appointment for me to see the same doctor, but I had to wait three months. So I was very happy to see her the next day. When she saw the lesion on my back from my penicillin sensitivity, she blurted out, "Beautiful! I never saw this type of reaction before." She then examined my foot and placed some blue liquid on it and said to me, "If this doesn't work, nothing else will." The next morning, I jumped out of bed as usual to prepare for work. When my foot touched the floor, I fell flat on my face from the excruciating pain I felt. Nervously, I looked at my foot, and it appeared as if it were on fire. I never thought in my life that I would appreciate pain the way I did at that moment because I realized I was regaining life in my foot once again, and I praised God above. Within one week, my foot was completely healed. There was a good older friend of my wife who lived in the apartment above and who was diabetic. She had a sore on her leg that would never heal, and all the doctors could do for her was to bandage the leg. She changed bandages for over twenty years and was kept indoors for that period of time. Seeing what the treatment did for me, I told my wife to apply the liquid to her leg, and amazingly, healing took place within one week. The other succeeding week, she was out on the streets after twenty years.

Back to work at the abattoir, I encountered members of Jim Jones commune in the form of a bevy of beautiful women. Initially, Jones had come to Guyana to help develop the government's agricultural program. With that initial visit, he had suffered a setback with his arrangements with the government because of his actions at one of his church meetings. He had presented himself as a faith healer joining a list of other faith healers who visited Guyana. But when he placed his hand into the mouth of one member of the congregation who had stood up and claimed to be suffering from cancer and pulled the cancer out and held it up in his hands, everyone, to his surprise, knew something was wrong. The so-called cancer-suffering individual was one of his members whom he had planted in the congregation pretending to be a local person from the community. After that incident, he had left Guyana but returned some six months later to set up his so-called commune in the hinterland of Guyana near the Venezuela border.

The bevy of beauties went to the abattoir to get acquainted with the butchers to make arrangements to ship meat into the commune which was stationed near the border with Venezuela. I had gotten very acquainted with these women because I was able to use their vehicle to do my field work (the government could not have afforded to give their officers vehicles to do their fieldwork). I was amazed how organized they were when I visited their headquarters in the capital city (Georgetown) of Guyana. There, they were taking care of handicapped children, which included schooling from kindergarten level. My thoughts still lingered on the time when that individual, suffering from hypothermia after his escape from Jonestown, was brought into the hospital where I was a patient. The "inquisitive minds want to know" situation was realized when I was asked by the Ministry of Agriculture Veterinary Division to go into the commune to determine the agriculture needs of the members of the Jim Jones cult. On my arrival in the area (accompanied by an inspector of police who traveled with me but was asked not to disclose his identity), I asked the station police commander for an escort into the commune. Without any hesitation, I was told that the area was off-limits and no one was allowed to visit. I told the commander that I was on an assignment from the Ministry of Agriculture and I intended to satisfy that assignment. "Well, you can go in at your own risk," was his reply. I obtained a vehicle with a driver from the agricultural outpost and was on my way. On arrival at the site, a large semicircular sign "The People's Temple" stood in front of me at the entrance that had a military outpost. I introduced myself to the guard and was told that he had to request a special vehicle to take me into the commune but couldn't say how long it would take. Being the firm and aggressive person that I am, I told him that this is my country and I was on assignment from the Ministry of Agriculture and I don't have time to waste. On impulse, I walked past the outpost and headed on foot with my heavy field veterinary kit in my hand toward the command center which was about three miles from the outpost.

The Peoples Temple Center was in the middle of the jungle. It had a breathtaking kind of view. The dirt road pathway was lined with banana trees swaying in the wind. But underneath that picturesque view, there was some sort of misery. As I continued with my walk, I heard strange noises like machetes cutting through grass. I parted some of the banana trees and saw a slavery-type scenery with guards overlooking some members hacking away at the grassland, trying to make a clear pathway. Along the dirt road,

I encountered a wide ditch that only a large high-powered truck could cross over. This was created to trap any vehicle that managed to bypass the guards. I eventually tracked into the commune after what seemed to be a gruesome three-mile walk. Seeing my visit was an unexpected one, I was able to witness the natural type of environment within the commune. I was greeted by Jim Jones and introduced to the members of his family, which consisted of many adopted adult sons and a couple of his biological children. It was obvious that some of his sons were not pleased by my unexpected visit, but he was very excited to have me.

The tour of the commune began with a visit to his agriculture animal farm project, which was very impressive at first impression. The farm consisted mainly of cattle, pigs, and poultry. Next, a tour of the housing project was even more impressive. These were very attractive houses for accommodation of the commune members. Most impressive was the nursery. There were over two hundred babies being attended for most efficiently in a jungle environment. Many rural hospital administrators would have envied that type of set up. Everything was surprisingly clean. During the tour, I asked to use the bathroom and was left dumbfounded at what I saw for a pith toilet. This toilet would have compared with any in a mansion. It was sealed off like a housed bathroom with an attractive entrance. There were a couple of tall trees surrounding the toilet seat, and the whistling of the birds would have made any constipated person relieved from that discomforting feeling. About half an hour in my sightseeing, it was obvious that something was wrong. Some members of the commune were walking around as if nothing existed around them.

I was invited to a meeting whereby, in my opinion, he wanted to show off his commitment to his teaching of socialism because Guyana had a socialist government at that time. There, he stood bellowing out questions of his socialist teachings to his congregation, which consisted of members between ten and one hundred years of age. The oldest person was the one who failed to answer his question correctly. She was so gripped with fear that she stumbled, and his facial expression angrily changed to one of disappointment. After that session, I was invited to a "long table" conference where all his sons and commune administrators were seated to discuss matters relating to the day's activities. This brought some opposition from one of his adopted sons who made it quite clear that he didn't want me sitting in at the meeting. At that instant, I indicated to Jim Jones that it was getting late and it was time for me to leave. "You don't have to leave. You can overnight," he remarked to me excitedly. "No, he cannot overnight!" This was the exclamatory remark from one of his adopted sons. An argument pursued between Jim Jones and this so-called son of his, to the extent that I had to intervene once again and declared that I would leave.

My departure from Jones Town was incident-free. At that time, I had the experience of riding in a massive truck that gave me a good bumping around. During the journey, my conversation with the driver had convinced me that many things weren't right in the commune. He was a somewhat-young veteran who had served in Vietnam, and along with other veterans, according to him, they were there to protect the commune from the United States government.

The next day, as I was waiting at the airport to get to the next plane out of the area, Jim Jones turned up with his team to collect supplies that were flown in from Georgetown, the capital city. That was a very uncomfortable situation for me because during my visit, I was accompanied by an inspector of police from the police headquarters in Georgetown, but he was in plain clothes during the visit. Now he was well-dressed in his police uniform as he stood beside me, and I didn't want Jones to suspect that we had come into his commune to spy on him.

The following day, I was back to work as usual, dealing with the corruption at the abattoir and working with farmers who were the only honest individuals that I was exposed to. Many times, I was accompanied on my farm trips by members of Jim Jones commune (all females) who were stationed in Georgetown as administrators. During one of these trips, I became very disturbed while having a conversation with about six members who made up the group. They indicated that they had to return home and would not be able to accompany me anymore on my farm trips. My response was "When would you all be leaving for California?" Because they had all come from that state, so when they mentioned "home," I assumed they were referring to that state. "No! Home is in Jonestown, not California," one of them replied quite proudly. As I looked among the group, they were all sad faces. I asked myself, "Why the sad faces?" This became apparent the next week. After the farm trip, they let me off at the agriculture head office where we said goodbye.

One afternoon during the next week after saying goodbye, while relaxing at home and listening to the British Broadcasting Corporation (BBC) news, which came over the airways at 4:15 every afternoon, I heard the tragic news of a massive suicide at Jonestown. "So this is what they meant when they told me they had to go home," I said to myself. *So many beautiful women knowing and willingly going to their deaths*, was a further thought of mine. Up to this day, the memories of those fine women still haunt me.

As the months went by, I continued trying to deal with the corruption within the abattoir and the police department. I had gained the support of the assistant chief officer in charge of proceedings at the abattoir. He indicated to me his admiration of my efforts to see things go right at the abattoir. He then offered his help to assist me in any way possible. That offer resulted in his demise. One bright and breezy evening after leaving work, he stopped me and asked to join him in an invited drink with the boss man rustler and his criminal cronies. Right away, I refused and advised him to do the same. But he said that he was willing to let bygones be bygones, so I decided to join them just to hear what they had to say.

The chief veterinary officer called me into his office one day for a brief conference and asked me to be prepared to go to the Dominican Republic to attend a two-week conference on African swine fever. This is a disease of major economic significance for most developing countries that depend on agriculture for their existence and pork accounted for about 80 percent of that country's exports. A declaration of an outbreak by the government would have resulted in a ban on all pork and pork products from that country, which would have actually crippled it economically. The disease acquired epidemic proportion in that country for political advantage by the failure of the government to admit an outbreak. The conference was only to be attended by veterinarians from different countries throughout the Western Hemisphere. The Food and Agriculture Organization of the United Nations sponsored the program and invited two veterinarians from each country. I was just an animal health assistant at that time. At the school I attended, most of the instructors were veterinarians from many different countries, and most of the subject material for a veterinary program were taught. After graduation, my performance in the field was outstanding; for example, when I did a cesarean section on a cow in the field, that animal would live, but when done by the veterinarian, that cow would die. Coupled with my surgical skills were my management skills, which were lacking in many veterinarians. One such veterinarian who was trained in England and believed he was superior to other veterinarians trained in other countries displayed his lack of surgical knowledge when he castrated (neutered) a dog using the procedure for a male piglet (small pig). This pet was a beautiful German Shepherd. The pet was hemorrhaging so much after the procedure, and he became confused to the extent that he didn't know what to do. Luckily for him, I appeared on the scene and had to tell him what to do to stop the hemorrhaging. There was another case involving this same veterinarian. He examined a cow that was pregnant and told the farmer that the cow wasn't pregnant. The next morning, the cow gave birth. In another case, another veterinarian who had claimed to have multiple degrees in veterinary medicine condemned a herd of prolific Barbados black sheep and indicated that they were genetically incapable of being prolific. I was summoned by the chief veterinary officer to take these so-called genetically deficient sheep to an area monitored by the police department to await slaughter. Under my guidance, they were instructed how to manage the sheep. The result was that the sheep were nutritionally but not genetically deficient. With the right feeding and deworming practices, within six months, they became reproductively prolific. Again, because of the incompetence of a veterinarian, I was asked by the chief veterinary officer to go into the hinterland of Guyana to a cattle ranching area called the Rupununi to investigate the spread of a devastating economically disabling disease called Foot and Mouth. As it turned out, the spread was caused by the veterinarian who didn't know that driving his vehicle from the infected herd to other healthy herds would result in the spread of the disease. In another situation, I was summoned once again by the chief veterinary officer to travel at that time to an area called Ebini in the Berbice county area to investigate the mounting mortality rate of sheep over the past couple of years. Experts from the United States and other parts of the world were summoned to solve the problem without any positive result. As it turned out, a couple of samples of toxic weed growing among the grass resulted in the toxicity of these animals. Again, an investigation from a report made by a rich individual (who bought over three hundred head of dairy cattle) about the district veterinarian who couldn't solve his problem. His problem was that he couldn't get any milk from any of the animals that were about two years of age. After all types of treatments from the district veterinarian without out any result, the case was referred to me. As it turned out, the animals were all heifers (virgins) and would only be able to produce milk after becoming pregnant and giving birth to calves. So he was advised to purchase dairy bulls for the herd. Further, I was called on by the wife of the president of Guyana to troubleshoot all their veterinary and management problems. Also, the mounted branch of the police department relied on my advice and veterinary care of their horses.

The culminating effect of my demonstrative knowledge of therapeutic and management practices in the livestock industry resulted in me being the first choice to attend the conference in the Dominican Republic on diagnostic and preventive procedures for African swine fever. My first choice selection by the chief veterinary officer caused an uproar among the veterinarians. They strongly contested my selection on the grounds that the conference was only for veterinarians. But the chief veterinary officer was more interested in the person he could have depended on to prevent the spread of the disease into Guyana. The most vocal of the veterinarians was the one who fooled the government initially about his postdoctoral degrees in veterinary medicine. His challenge was met with an assignment for both of us in the Interior of Guyana in a livestock management area called Ibini. There, we had to do some blood sampling of some buffaloes. My sample take was twice that of his within the same time period. The event was witnessed by visiting foreign veterinarians, which made the situation quite embarrassing for him. On our return to the city, I had a state car awaiting my arrival, while the visiting colleagues and himself had to await their own transportation which was uncertain about the arrival time. So he asked one of the other officers if he could have gotten a ride with my transportation; the officer told him he had to ask me, which was an additional embarrassment for him.

The assistant department head was the other choice. This was a guy who relished in receiving produce from farmers as compensation for his services. He was an Indian national who wasn't interested in the country's welfare, only his own, but he was a pleasantly nice guy and, in my opinion, used his position to go on the trip. So the morning of our departure, this guy had all the tourist camera equipment slung over his shoulders. I said to myself that he is definitely going on a sightseeing trip. As we made our way onto the tarmac to board the plane, there was a reception committee of the police band that was there to welcome the visiting president of Venezuela. The band struck up its welcoming notes while we were on the tarmac because the president's plane was about to land, but Dr. Raj thought the welcoming committee was for him; so much for self-image.

We were late on arrival in the Dominican Republic, and much of the taxi traffic had left. So transportation was difficult to get because neither of us spoke Spanish. There was some type of warning about the disease at the airport. Dr. Raj spotted the word *veterinario* and said to me with his Indian accent, "Rillen, man, Spanish is easy. I am certain that word means veterinarian." I replied, "Probably so, but that's just one Spanish word that looks English." He said, "Let me show you," and hailed a taxi driver with the word *veterinario*, who came running toward us. When he saw the guy's response, he said to me, "I told you, Spanish is easy." When the taxi driver came up closer, he said to him, "*Veterinario wanto goeo hotelio.*" The taxi driver initially smiled when he heard the word *veterinario* but then changed his expression to one of utter amazement with the other words. Dr. Raj also became puzzled when the taxi driver didn't understand his other Spanish words and said surprisingly to me, "Rillen, man, that guy don't know Spanish. Let's try another guy." I said to him, "Dr. Raj, believe me, all the Spanish-speaking guys in the world wouldn't understand your Spanish."

The first day of the conference started with some concern for me which was twofold. First, my mode of dress was revolutionary. It was stated by the organizers that all dress had to be formal (shirt and tie/jacket), but I was clad in Guyana's national wear, which was designed for comfort because of the hot climate. It was known as the shirt jack. All eyes were on me, seeing that my appearance was different, and discriminatory comments were made by the other attendees. It so turned out that the hotel's gift shop had a similar shirt on display, and when the afternoon session resumed, about 90 percent of the attendees were wearing the shirt. The other concern was that tables with name tags were set for each country's representatives. On my approach to the Guyana's delegation table, I saw my name listed as doctor. It should have been mister because, at that time, I wasn't a veterinarian. However, the conference was only for veterinarians, so the organizers were expecting only veterinarians. But as was mentioned previously, Guyana was only interested in whom they could depend on to take on the job of preventing the spread of the disease into the country. After taking my seat, I looked around for the other Guyana delegate who was nowhere to be seen. As I was pummeled with questions about his whereabouts, he was sightseeing. The conference was for about two weeks, and he probably attended about two sessions. So the onus was on me to collect every detail about this disease. Further, I decided that I had to show myself as a worthy representative of Guyana.

A group of pigs were injected with the African swine fever virus, and after about five days of the incubation period, an autopsy/necropsy was performed to show the effects of various lesions as they occur on the animals' organs. A United States Department of Agriculture (USDA) professor was in charge of the proceedings. While he was performing the necropsy, he was describing the lesions for the group as part of the teaching process. I said to myself, "This professor cannot remember everything about the disease, so he is entitled to make a mistake." By the time that thought cleared my mind, he made that mistake, and I pounced on that opportunity to correct him. The mistake was that he referred to a parasitic lesion that occurs in pigs as a tapeworm when, in fact, it was the cyst of the tapeworm that occurs in humans who become infected when undercooked pork is ingested. Everyone kept quiet as we exchanged friendly words about the problem which was an incidental one and not related to the actual disease. After agreeing with me about the mistake he made and correcting himself, I kind of became the talk of the conference.

The conference was concluded with a dinner, and at that time, the organizers insisted that everyone must be formally dressed in suit and tie. Dr. Raj came to me to inquire about my attire for that evening. I told him that I would be wearing my national attire, which was designed like the casual wear but with a more formal appearance of a suit but cannot be worn with a tie. He told me that he had a similar outfit and would be wearing that too. As I approached the dinner hall where everyone had gathered, I heard loud laughter. When I entered the hall, I saw Dr. Raj among others laughing at himself. Yes! Dr. Raj was really laughing at himself while the others were laughing at him. He looked like the perfect clown dressed in his casual shirt jack and wearing a tie. No one knew that there was a shirt jack suit that I was wearing. All eyes were now on me with admiration as I sauntered my way along. The suit was immaculately made and fitted me the same way. Then all the laughter changed to admiration.

Back in Guyana, I was given the responsibility by the Ministry of Agriculture to prepare and monitor all measures to prevent the disease from entering Guyana. That was in addition to my responsibilities at the abattoir and attending to the needs of my district farmers. On my return visit to the abattoir, I noticed that Scottie, the assistant public health officer who had offered to help me stamp out the corruption at the abattoir and who had that drink with the boss man rustler, was not present. On inquiry, I was told that he was hospitalized a couple of days after having that drink, which was about the same time I had left the country for the conference. Further inquiries indicated that he would have relapses after feeling better for a couple of days. When I heard this, I became very concerned because those are some of the symptoms of slow poisoning. Two weeks later, Scottie died. I knew at that time it was that drink he had taken with the boss man rustler that I had warned him about taking. To prove my suspicions, after the funeral, I invited the boss man henchmen (four of them) for a drink. They were suspicious initially because they knew I didn't drink. But I know a regular drinker of alcohol wouldn't refuse a drink. Growing up, it was always said that what a sober mind conceals a drunken mind reveals. So the idea was to get them intoxicated before I asked the question "Who killed Scottie?" When the time was right, I asked that question, and the results were amazing. Simultaneously, four voices said, "Not me, vet. It was the boss man!" At that time, they wanted to know what I was going to do about their confession. I responded, "All I wanted to do was to confirm my suspicions," and left it at that.

The preparations to implement the preventive measures for African swine fever in Guyana became very demanding, resulting in me leaving the abattoir. This was great news for the boss man rustler because he could resort back to his old ways of bribery of corrupt government officers.

The chief veterinary officer heard of my plans to apply for a government scholarship to go overseas to study veterinary medicine. He didn't approve of my plans, so he decided to make me an offer to become an agriculture officer (this position required the qualification of a bachelor's degree in animal science which I didn't have) in one of the unmanageable areas in the agriculture department. He indicated that being a strong person, I would have been the ideal person for the position. But I indicated to him that all my interest was in becoming a veterinarian. So I proceeded to apply for the scholarship. The application had to go through his office for him to sign off on it. Now all scholarship awardees had to do a stint of military service. After one year had passed and not hearing from the government, I decided to go to the office that processed the applications to make inquiries. There, I was made to understand that the application was not submitted. At that time, I realized that efforts to become a veterinarian would meet with major obstacles. So I prepared myself for a tough fight, knowing that my competence in my work was to become one of the obstacles in my way. I always believed that as long as one has faith in God, with hard work, you can achieve anything in life. Applications for government scholarships are only accepted once per year within a certain time period. It so happened that at that time the next year, the chief veterinary officer had left the country on government business, and during his absence, the assistant chief was appointed as acting chief veterinary officer. So I filled out the application, took it to him, and told him the chief veterinary officer said before he left the country on government business that he must sign the application. Without hesitation, he signed it. I immediately took the application and submitted it personally to the relevant government agency. Within one week, I heard from the government inviting me to do the stint of military service as a prerequisite to being offered the scholarship.

The journey into the militarized zone in the interior of Guyana was adventurous. A World War Two landing craft was made available to sail with a packed boat of pioneers and a couple of pigs across the Atlantic Ocean into the interior region of Guyana. The journey was supposed to take twelve hours but took three days. Initially, everyone was in good spirits and made sure to keep away from the pigs. Conversations erupted to pass the time. This particular guy who was Muslim by religion boasted that under no condition would he ever eat meat. So one can imagine how far away he kept from the pigs on board.

Six hours into the journey, the captain miscalculated, took the wrong turn, and was heading for Trinidad. Realizing his mistake, he threw the anchor to get his coordinates right. We spent an additional three days at sea without any food. The entire boat was rocking with seasick pioneers. Many of us found ourselves lying among the pigs but were too weak to move.

The sight of the land and the docking of that memorable landing craft was welcomed by everyone because that meant that we were nearing our destination. Somehow or other, many of us found the energy to jump on the waiting train, while others made it aboard on their knees. There was an additional sixty miles to be traveled to a site to join a couple of trucks to make the final run. The train rolled on the tracks at about ten miles per hour, much to the disgust of everyone. We were told if it traveled faster, it would have run off the tracks. Six hours later, we made it to the site of the waiting trucks, but there were no trucks. It was about 8:00 that evening, with an additional ten miles to travel to the military center. All the pioneers, except me, decided that they will walk the ten miles. You see, I never follow a crowd unless I am acquainted with the environment, and no one had such an acquaintance. So I decided to sit by the roadside on my suitcase, hoping that a truck would pass by for me to hitch a ride. About one hour into my waiting, the manager from the hotel up the street passed by, saw me sitting on my suitcase, and inquired of my situation, which I sadly lamented to her. She then invited me to stay in the hotel free of cost, allowing me to have a good night's rest. About 6:00 the next morning, I was able to hitch a ride on a truck. Along the way, the truck was picking up pioneers lying by the roadside.

The military center was a welcomed site. The sergeant major was waiting for our arrival. We were greeted with many cauldrons of hot food, but my boasting Muslim friend was not that happy because all the food was cooked with meat. He appealingly asked the sergeant major for food without meat, who harshly replied to him, "What you see is what you get." My Muslim friend picked up his plate, went over to the cauldron, dished out the food, and started to eat. Then I looked at him and said, "Never say never," reminding him of his words when we were traveling on the boat that under no circumstance would he ever eat meat.

The situation at the military base was a trying one for me. I am not one to tolerate shouts from anyone. "How am I going to cope with the military commands?" I kept asking myself. Controlling my temper was the key for me to finish my military stint to obtain that government scholarship to become a veterinarian. I realized my problem was genetic and the key was to avoid a situation that would trigger this dreaded reaction. But as long I was in the military, I would be subjected to the normal military behavior of shouts and insults by the training officers. After surviving two days of training without being shouted at but witnessing the verbal abuse thrown at other recruits, I realized it was just a matter of time before my turn came along. So I turned to my spiritual belief and asked for guidance, and amazingly, almost everything fell into place. On my way to the barracks the second afternoon after training, I observed a stench which turned out to be coming from the poultry pens (the military base had an agriculture unit to be self-sufficient with meat production). What I saw was a highly insanitary environment with birds that were black in color but were supposed to be white. I immediately asked to see the commanding officer who was glad to see me to discuss the problem when he learned of my veterinary background. Immediately, I was placed in charge of the agriculture unit and was exempted from the drill square training. My appointment by the commanding officer started to create some interpersonal problems with the officer who was in charge of the unit. He claimed he had a degree in animal science, which superseded my qualification. So my response to the commanding officer was that his qualification was on paper, but not with his knowledge, and the poor management of the farm was living proof. But to be fair,

I was willing to test his knowledge at another level. That morning, I had scheduled the castration of six large boars. He was to do half of the castrations. After completing my half of the castrations, I asked about his whereabouts because he didn't do his half of the job. He was nowhere to be seen on the center again. The lesson is not to doubt anyone about his/her claims; just put that individual to the test.

Cleaning up the mess on the agriculture unit didn't take long. Further, to ensure maintenance of the unit when my stint was over, I embarked on a training program for other pioneers, which pleased the major overwhelmingly.

The other part of my training was to be done at the head office in the city. This pleased me a great deal because I didn't have to worry about my family anymore; while in the military, there was no communication with them for months. At the office, I was given the task of doing clerical work and was under the supervision of the assistant director general for agriculture and a major with a degree in animal science. This type of degree offers information more in the management aspect of livestock, not in diagnostics and treatment of livestock, which is the veterinarian's job and which my training as an animal health assistant had given me much knowledge of to perform veterinary duties as mentioned previously. The major was a friend to me because he wanted to get as much veterinary information from me, but the director general (DG) was an arrogant, mister-know-it-all type of individual. He believed he was an expert in every profession, and veterinary medicine was no exception because he, too, had a degree in animal science. But as demonstrated before with the officer and the castration of the pigs, I like to put individuals to the test when they claim to know much about nothing in my field of work. So I decided to let the DG know how limited his knowledge was in veterinary medicine because no one can be a jack of all trades and be efficient in a specified professional area of work. So one day, a report came in from the military center about some cows becoming sick. Immediately, the DG came up with his diagnosis of brucellosis, which is a disease of many animals that causes abortion in them and is contagious to humans, commonly known as undulant fever. Some blood samples were taken and sent to the veterinary laboratory at the Ministry of Agriculture. I called the veterinarian in charge and told him I wanted a technical report with all the veterinary terminology. The major received the report and immediately took it to the DG. Thirty minutes later, the major summoned me to his office to ask what the report meant. "Didn't you give the report to the DG?" I asked the major. "Yes!" he responded. "And?" was my short inquiry. "He asked me to interpret it, and I told him I couldn't, that he will have to ask you." When I went to DG's office, he humbly asked me in a soft tone of voice to interpret the laboratory results. Firstly, I told him that his diagnosis was miles away from what the animals were suffering from, and secondly, I told him the truth, that I purposely requested the report to be written in that format to prove to him his deficient knowledge in veterinary medicine.

In the month of March 1981, I received a letter from the government granting me a scholarship to study veterinary medicine. On the other hand, that was just the beginning of a series of bigger problems that followed for me to bear and conquer. First, I was asked to submit the name of a guarantor to cover the cost of my training to ensure my return to Guyana. Most of my relatives, including my mom, had left Guyana for the United States. I had no one to turn to for any assistance. The home that I grew up in was willed to my eldest brother by my mom; she did that as a form of compensation for the sacrifice he made when he had to leave school at an early age to help her provide for eight other siblings. As I said earlier in my writing, I always turn to prayer when a situation seems hopeless. There was this female individual who was from England and met and married a Guyanese professional who returned to Guyana. She decided to start a poultry farm without much knowledge of animal husbandry. She lost a lot of her flock after seeking the help of many veterinarians. No one could have solved her problem until one day, I was asked to go to her farm by the Ministry of Agriculture. I worked with her and solved her problem which was related to poor management. Her number 1 problem was inadequate space for the number of birds (overcrowding), which led to an increase concentration of pathogens within the pen, thereby overcoming the birds' immunity, resulting in disease outbreaks. After that experience, I was the only one she called on for help. It was during one of my visits when she saw me looking somewhat melancholic and asked what my problem was. I mentioned that I had gotten a government scholarship but was finding difficulty meeting the government's terms of providing a guarantor. Without hesitation, she looked at me and said, "You will be a great veterinarian. Don't worry, I will stand guarantor for you." Once again, help had come to me from out of the blue. With my faith in God above rising high and not wanting to impose on the offer by the Guyanese professional's wife, I decided to write the government for a waiver of the guarantor requirement. Lo and behold, it was granted. As it turned out, I was the only one to obtain a waiver of all obligations to the government.

The Guyana government went into an economic slump in 1980, and some of the scholarships granted had to be redirected to Cuba because of the low/no cost of training to the Guyana government by the Cuban government. Knowing how things are with me, I figured that I would be one of the individuals to get the hammer. My scholarship was originally earmarked for the United States, but when I was told by the secretary to the office of the Public Service Ministry that I had to travel to Cuba to complete my studies, I knew that I had to find a way to reverse that decision. At that time, Guyana was a socialist country, and the word *comrade* when used as a form of addressing someone indicated that, that person was a supporting member of the ruling government. (Personally, I wasn't involved with any political party, but I used whatever was available to me to my advantage.) So that word, when used, made many people nervous. In my personal file, it was listed that I attended to the president's farm with his buffaloes. With a cold and hoarse voice, I said to the secretary, "Comrade, do you know who I am?" Immediately, her facial countenance changed to one of total surprise. She finally said, "We will see what we can do. Come back tomorrow." The next day, I was given the okay for travel to the United States. The following week, I went to pick up my check from another government office to leave the country. At that time, I was told that no money was available for me to leave on schedule. Again, the magic word *comrade* was used, and I got the same positive result. The money suddenly appeared from out of nowhere for me to travel. The next week, I arrived at the airport and boarded the Guyana Airways plane for travel to the United States. The plane was taxing when it was ordered to return the boarding area. At that time, I said to myself, "Lord, what evil I have to overcome now." It turned out that the situation had nothing to do with me, much to my relief.

I arrived at the Montgomery Regional Airport in Alabama in August 1981 to the welcome of no one, just my suitcase and I not knowing where I would sleep that night and other nights. With the help of the taxi driver, I found a hotel to lay my tiresome body on its warm comforting bed.

The day of my registration into the pre-veterinary program allowed for me to experience my first culture shock. While waiting in line to be registered, a male student called out to a female student, "Hey, bitch! Come here." She willingly replied, "Okay, Johnny, I am coming." My response was "What the hell? These guys don't have any respect for each other." After that initial cultural experience, the other one followed quickly. The next week during a break from classes, I witnessed some female students drinking alcohol and smoking, knowing that in Guyana, females seen drinking and smoking are labeled as prostitutes. This led to my statement to my fellow male students, "Guys, I didn't know prostitutes go to college in America." What I said, of course, brought great laughter.

During my first year in college, I witnessed cheating to an intolerable extent. This was strange to me because during my initial schooling in Guyana, the punishment for cheating was severe, and if you were planning to further your studies, this had to be done overseas. Any record of cheating prevented anyone from having that opportunity, so all work was done honestly. So when I was approached by a female class member with the request to sit next to me during an exam to get my answers because she didn't prepare for it, I used some cruel words to her. The cheating became so disgustingly unbearable that, during one physiology exam, I witnessed the professor leaving the examination room when he saw some students cheating. After the examination, I went to his office and asked him why he didn't challenge those students for cheating. He mentioned that he couldn't. I asked why. He said that the school's administration was always subject to lawsuit settlements, not being able to prove the case. On the other hand, some of the students who didn't cheat thought they were inferior to the cheating ones mentally because they didn't know they cheated to get good grades. The fact that black students felt they were inferior mentally to white students because they get better grades troubled me. So to prove the point, I personally set out to do some investigation of my own. I believed that no one who finished an exam in fifteen minutes that I took an hour to complete isn't on the level. First, I decided to observe the behavior of the white students. I found out that they obtained the identical exams from the secretaries, which they purchased from them. With this information, I chided the black students about their inferiority complex. They challenged me to take the information to the administration. I had to let them know that I wasn't in school for that purpose. Further, the administration already knew about the problem, but their hands were tied to do anything about it because of the students' lawsuits, which cost the school a bundle, knowing it is a private institution. I just wanted them to know that no one is smarter than the other based on the color of their skin. It's the dedication/discipline, commitment, religious fortitude, and belief in oneself that count. In addition to the gross cheating, the use of hard drugs by most students seem to be customary. I am convinced that the alarming increase in suicides among professionals stem from their addiction when they were in college.

May 10, 1987, was the date of my graduation from veterinary school. It was supposed to be a happy day for me, but that wasn't the case. One week before graduation, I was summoned to the financial office to be told that I couldn't graduate because my scholarship sponsor owed the school $3,000. My misfortunes in life have been so many that I have gotten accustomed to them, but in another way, I am lucky for my faith in God. In some kind of way, there was always some little doubt because in every situation of asking for his help, it always seemed impossible. I said to myself, "So many years of hard work and sacrifice and not being able to graduate because being in an intense professional school like veterinary medicine with a family of four to provide for took a lot of sacrificing." I appealed to the administration to allow me to pay off the amount after graduation, but they refused; they had to get their money. Two days before graduation, while walking down the street and pondering my future, I walked past a bank. Then the thought struck me, *Why not the bank?* Then another thought was *No! This is Alabama. I am a foreigner, black with bad credit. Racism is high in this state. All the banks are owned by whites. It isn't possible.* Somehow or other, I found myself in the bank. Among the many loan officers, there was one black person. I said to myself, "It would be nice if I can see this guy," because interviews were conducted sequentially. I don't know if he saw the melancholic look on my face and, at that moment, assessed my situation, but with the wave of his hand, he beckoned me to his office. I took the seat he offered and told him about my situation. Without hesitation, he took out his pen and wrote me a check for $3,000 and said, "Go and graduate. You can pay the bank back when you get a job." I became so emotional, I nearly forgot to thank him; I was mainly concerned with thanking God above for answering my prayers once again. By the time the administration had finished all the paperwork for my graduation, the time had passed. So a special ceremony was held for me to take the veterinary oath. That made me feel kind of special.

My first experience in the field of my profession as a veterinarian was quite stunningly disappointing. I was recruited by one of the school's alumni from rural Mississippi who was in practice for about ten years. I decided on a rural practice because I was keen on learning, and the best way to learn a lot is from a bad situation/environment. That veterinarian was held in high esteem by the community but was very unprofessional and a corrupt individual. Initially, this guy projected a friendship that was very helpful. He invited me into his home and allowed me to stay there for a while. During that time, I asked myself, "Why is this guy being so nice to me. I just got to meet him for the first time. There has to be something behind all of this." He also got me a very nice house to rent from one of his associates. With my suspicions of his behavior, I reflected on one of my mom's teachings: "Beware of the smiling and generous person." The veterinarian's generosity toward me was later perceived for me to keep quiet if and/or when I noticed his corrupt and incompetent attitude. Initially, he asked me one Sunday, "Doc, do you go to church?" I replied, "No! But that doesn't mean I am not a Christian." "Well, you have to go to church to get business for your clinic." I thought quietly to myself, *So this guy's churchgoing appearances are a sham,*" for I never heard him mention God's name. Further, I was asked by him to vaccinate a herd of cows against brucellosis, a disease transmissible to humans, causing a serious illness known as undulant fever. I called him up and told him he didn't have enough vaccine for all the cows. His remark stunned me, "Doc, inject them with water. She wouldn't know the difference." I was speechless. This guy had no knowledge of the public health implications if some infected animals were shipped out of state. Besides the public health issue, there were also the economic/production factors to be considered in terms of morbidity, mortality cases, and tracing the origin of a possible outbreak. Again, this guy would sell his clients' pets and tell them that the pets died. Then he would contract workers to do a job either at his home or his clinic and deny he ever told them to do much of the work so he wouldn't have to pay them. His corruption got intolerable when he started to steal some of his clients' cattle and place them on his farm. At that time, I decided that I had to find a way to dissociate myself from this guy because, according to the saying, "Show me your friends and I will tell you who you are."

During one of our clinic days, while he was administering fluids to a sick pet, he said to me, "Doc, I cannot understand why animals die whenever I give them fluids." After seeing how he was administering the fluids to the pet, I said to him, "Doc! You are drowning the pet. You are giving too much too quickly." After that, we had a discussion about fluid replacement and maintenance based on the level of the pet's hydration status (percentage of dehydration). Like many other medical professionals (human and veterinary medicine), his ability to calculate the dose of medication was appalling, more so for surgery. His way was by trial and error. If the pet died from the anesthesia, he knew he had given too much, and if the pet woke up during surgery, he knew he hadn't given enough. He preferred the latter for he knew if he didn't give enough, he could have always given a bit more without comprising the pet's life. Yet another case of professional misconduct in the form of cruelty to an animal was brought to my attention. This particular veterinarian was presented a canine pet for euthanasia. The animal was taken into the examination room for the procedure to be performed while the owner remained in the waiting room. After about fifteen minutes of waiting, the owner decided to go into the exam room and, to his surprise, saw the veterinarian choking the pet to end his life. Seeing this, the owner asked, "Doc! Is this the way animals are put to sleep?" In this case, the veterinarian became frustrated after many attempts of trying to find the vein without any success.

Dissociating myself from this veterinarian was one of the best things I had done. After witnessing the gross health problems among individuals in the community that were being associated with livestock and pets, I decided I needed postdoctoral training to be a complete and competent veterinarian. So I decided to reenter school to do a master's program in veterinary public health.

My program was initiated with a large dairy farm in Macon County, Alabama. The farmer had many years of unsolved health problems among his calves. Therefore, this was the appropriate farm to work on. I wanted my work to identify a problem and then solve it. I hypothesized that the food poisoning organism salmonella was the cause of the sick and dying calves. Now, for years, salmonella has always been known to exist in the poultry industry, primarily with eggs, and not to be associated with the dairy industry. As it turned out, salmonella was responsible for the calves' illness through nursing, thereby contracting the disease from the mother (cow). The work was laborious, intense, and frustrating sometimes. The dean of the School of Veterinary Medicine, who was one of my panel advisers, wanted me to do a quick work with the sampling of food items from supermarkets. But I wanted to do an original work, which took more work and time to complete. As it turned out, I had to dismiss the dean from my panel of advisers because we weren't on the same page. This he took personally and decided to become vindictive. He refused to sign off on my thesis that was okay with the other panel professors. At that time, I reminded him that he had a boss whom I would have approached if he didn't give me a valid reason for not signing off on my thesis. This he refused to do, so I took the thesis to the provost who was his boss and explained the problem. The provost took a couple days to read the thesis and approve it and directed him to sign it. The lesson is, one does not have to be intimidated by higher authority once you know your rights.

In 1992, I graduated with my postdoctoral degree and returned to Lexington, Mississippi, and opened up the first clinic in the state as a veterinary public health clinic (Holmes County Animal Hospital and Veterinary Public Health Clinic). I gave radio interviews, so the community got first-hand/first-class public health information involving pets and livestock. The response was so overwhelming from the public that they were confronting me about treatment for themselves and their children, but sadly, I had to remind them that I only had a license to practice veterinary medicine. I realized that the medical doctors didn't have a clue about this type of medicine. Clients were reporting unresponsive diarrhea in their kids while in day care centers. This is a parasite (Giardia) of the intestinal tract that is common among children in day care centers. So through the local health community center, I managed to get individual interviews with some of the medical doctors. What perplexed me the most was that they couldn't have envisaged the serious health issues that could have arisen from those problems. What I referred to later as the classical demonstration of ignorance from a professional was when I met with the senior doctor of the health center. After expressing my concerns to him for members of the community and their children about the many parasitic infections, he looked at me straight in the eyes and, with confidential arrogance, said, "Those problems only occur in Africa and not in the United States." My response was "So when people from Africa come to this country with their children, what do they do? Do they leave the parasites at the airport?" After that comment, my final comment to him was "Where ignorance is bliss, it's folly to be wise." He had a look of amazement on his face because I knew he didn't understand my proverbial comment. Then I left his office. Definitely, this was one of the many professionals who had cheated his way through school.

Working in Lexington, Mississippi, with livestock and pets was a great experience. The many zoonoses (diseases transmissible from animals to man) are of major significance. It was and still is quite clear that the medical doctors do not have a clue about diagnosing these problems. So residents will continue to experience the poor quality of medicine that is being practiced relating to these problems.

In 1998, I experienced tremendous losses to my hospital/clinic because of a massive flood. That situation resulted in me leaving that area for New York in May 2001. Surprisingly, I was subjected to more racial slurs from white people in New York than when I was in Mississippi. While I was working with a reputable incorporated animal hospital in Staten Island, there was this white female client who told the receptionist, "I don't want that black doctor handling my animal." The next week, I was asked to leave the job. From then on, I sought of jobs in nonwhite areas. I must say that any racial individual is one that is mentally restricted and answers to the proverbial saying "Where ignorance is bliss, it's folly to be wise." So because off such gross ignorance of that person, he/she will never understand a situation when explained for the purpose of gaining knowledge.

My next employment was with an animal shelter. At that time, a personnel had asked me to sign a nondisclosure letter. This request aroused my suspicions about the shelter. After about one week of employment, the request to sign such a letter became quite apparent. Healthy animals were purposely provoked while eating to initiate aggression to justify their euthanasia. One day, I mentioned to the female manager (who seemed to get a kick out of this provocation) that if you provoke me while I am eating, I may also try to bite you. Further, young females were given the task to euthanized animals. That I found to be very disturbing. I finally reached the threshold of my tolerance when I saw one day, the female manager wrestling with a pit bull who was very bloody from the continuous jarring motion of a snare around his mouth. The disturbing part of this incident was that she was having fun with the animal's pain. I rebuked her about her actions, much to the annoyance of the administration. They called me up on the phone and reminded me of the nondisclosure letter I signed. This made me angry because they had no respect for my profession of preventing cruelty to animals. So I let them know that I didn't give a damn about the letter I signed because no details were laid out about cruelty to animals, which I should have tolerated when observed, and if that information was disclosed, no way would I have signed that letter. My objection to the inappropriate behavior of the shelter employees toward animals condoned by the administration and my refusal to keep quiet resulted in my resignation being asked for to leave the company.

I started working as a private veterinarian in the Bronx after leaving the shelter. Mainly, my work involves educating clients about how to keep their pets healthy and eventually themselves with information about diseases transmissible from animals to humans. There are many such diseases, mainly from internal and external parasites which are very common among pets. Look out for my next issue which contains information about many of the diseases that are transmissible from animals to man and man to animals and the preventive measures to implement. For veterinary and public health information, you can contact the writer, Dr. R. C. Rillen DVM, MS.

PHONE: 347-256-3016.
FAX: 347-529-3186
E-MAIL: drrillen947@yahoo.com

www.ingramcontent.com/pod-product-compliance
Lightning Source LLC
Chambersburg PA
CBHW020327130626
46549CB00003B/1057

9 7 8 1 9 6 7 3 6 2 8 4 4